THE LIMITS
OF ALTRUISM

THE
PATTEN
FOUNDATION

In 1931, Will Patten of Indianapolis (A.B., Indiana University, 1893) made a gift to his Alma Mater for the establishment of the Patten Foundation. Under the terms of this gift the Foundation brings to the campus scholars of eminence, who are in residence for several weeks during the academic year. Opportunities are thus provided for students, faculty, and friends of the University to enjoy the privilege and advantage of personal acquaintance with the visitors. The Patten Foundation Lecturer in the fall of 1976 was Professor Garrett Hardin.

THE LIMITS
OF ALTRUISM

An Ecologist's
View of Survival

GARRETT HARDIN

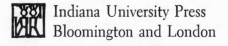 Indiana University Press
Bloomington and London

Published in Canada by Fitzhenry & Whiteside Limited, Don Mills, Ontario
Manufactured in the United States of America

Library of Congress Cataloging in Publication Data
Hardin, Garrett James, 1915–
The limits of altruism.
Includes bibliographical references and index.
1. Altruism.   2. Human ecology.   I. Title.
BF637.H4H37   1977   301.31   77-74451
ISBN 0-253-33435-7   1 2 3 4 5 81 80 79 78 77

CONTENTS

A Prologue of Paradoxes

IF YOU SAY, "I obey only egoistic impulses," I cannot prove you wrong; for if I ask, "Why did you help that person?" you have only to answer, "Because his warm smile made me feel good," and I cannot refute you. You can successfully maintain that you sought nothing more than your own pleasure.

I may counter this by asserting that I am often moved by pure altruism, the pure desire to help others. (*Alter* means "other" in Latin.) I may even insist that the good feelings I get from an altruistic act are no more than irrelevant by-products. Or I may say that they have this relevance: they are the signs whereby I recognize true altruism, which is my abiding passion.

A "waterproof hypothesis" is a hypothesis so worded that no observation can refute it. The trick is in the protective wording. Science does not admit invincible assertions into its sanctuary. Are the egoistic and altruistic positions no more than waterproof hypotheses?

Or must we look at these positions from the standpoint of gamesmanship (à la Potter)?

If I am a clever egoist I can profit by encouraging you to be altruistic. I will be happy to be an "other" for you to serve. But

I won't tell you this because you, as a doctrinaire altruist, may be unwilling to encourage egoists. So as a selfish, Machiavellian egoist it is against my interest to let you in on my secret. For me to reveal the egoist's secret would be to act altruistically.

Must an egoist, then, be forever silent about his motives? Worse: must he be a hypocrite and praise altruism? Among all those who praise altruism how am I to distinguish truth-tellers from hypocrites?

Appeal to me as an altruist and I will reply, "If I admit to being an altruist you will take advantage of me." (Ministers of religion are notoriously easy marks for shysters and salesmen.)

The outward face of commercialism is an altruistic face: "Free gift!" screams the banner erected by one who learned in school that there's no such thing as a free lunch. Competing screamers politely refrain from removing one another's masks. Those who have something to sell conspire silently to foster the illusion of altruism.

But is there anyone who does not have *something* to sell?

If you want me to do something for you, you must first convince me that it is to my egoistic advantage to take your advice. Having said that, must I not (to preserve symmetry in human relations) appeal in turn only to your egoism?

The Cardinal Rule of Policy is this: *Never ask a person to act against his own self-interest.* Thus do we show respect for one another.

Do you still have altruistic impulses? Splendid! But don't talk about them. Act them out—but not if you cannot enjoy what you are doing in silence. Enjoy! Enjoy!

Altruists who understand the total situation must live by a double standard: one code of ethics for their own actions, another for others'. They must ask for less than they are prepared to give.

Perhaps the most painful thing for the self-conscious altruist is the dilemma he faces: if he openly promotes altruism he encourages chicanery; but if no one talks about altruism at all, the impulse may wither away completely.

In the *reductio ad absurdum* of mathematics we first assume that which in the end leads to its own disproof. The dialectic of the gambit cannot be transfixed like an insect on a pin; elusive, it reappears time after time. Christ said, "Whosoever will lose his life for my sake shall find it," and left it to his hearers to figure out what he meant.

Two hundred years later Sextus Empiricus said, "It is not impossible for the man who has ascended to a high place by a ladder to overturn the ladder with his foot after his ascent." Wittgenstein, perhaps not aware of the origin of the image, concluded his *Tractatus* with almost the same words.

The assumption of pure egoism may not be enough to explain all human actions. If so, will we not discover this sooner by presuming that it is?

Strait is the way to truth. The path is not recommended to the faint of heart.

1

Does Altruism Exist?

MANY PEOPLE FEEL threatened by the question with which we begin. This point is well illustrated in a story told by Ernest Jones,[1] Freud's biographer. During a visit to the United States in 1909 Jones explained his master's views on dreams to a meeting of the American Psychological Association, emphasizing Freud's contention that dreams are always ego-centered. His assertion caused a lady in the audience to rise in indignant denial: she was perfectly willing to allow that the dreams of the *Viennese* might be egoistic but she was sure that *American* dreams were altruistic!

In its secondary sense *dream* means "daydream; reverie; aspiration." I am afraid we must admit that the indignant lady was right: the daydreams of "our best people" now are preponderently altruistic. Americans may not be unique in this, but I suspect we lead the crowd. As inheritors of the evangelical tradition and as a rich people who can afford to be generous, many of us are sure that altruism is as hardheaded a fact as egoism. We proudly cite the success of the Marshall Plan, through which we channeled $12 billion into Europe to help in its rebuilding after World War II. If what we did in Europe wasn't altruism, what is?

The Marshall Plan is as close to national altruism on a large scale as anything we can find. Even so, it is sufficiently ambiguous to illustrate an important point about altruism to which we will return repeatedly. The Marshall Plan was not *pure* altruism, if by that term we mean an act that benefits the "other" without benefiting the party of the first part. We were quite honest about this aspect of the Marshall Plan at the time, acknowledging that we wanted to help Europe so that we could keep our enemy, the Soviet Union, at bay. Altruism was mixed with national self-interest.

Pure altruism, by definition, does not benefit the actor; in its extreme form, it may even harm him. Does pure altruism exist? We can grant that any behavior, no matter how remarkable, must occur now and then. Mere existence is not the important question: what matters is persistence. Can altruistic behavior persist and increase, perhaps ultimately becoming the norm to which egocentric behavior is the exception? Such is the dream of compassionate people. Is it a realistic dream?

Our main interest is in the human species, but the groundwork for understanding altruism must be laid in general biology. Until about two hundred years ago it was widely supposed that God's great plan sometimes required that one species be designed to serve another. Especially was it presumed that other animals serve the needs of human beings: honeybees make honey *in order that* man may have something sweet to put on his bread. This homocentric view was fully developed by John Ray (1627–1705) in the first part of the eighteenth century. Before the century was out the Reverend William Paley (1743–1803) refuted Ray. Bees produce honey, he said, for their own needs; man merely takes advantage of their activities. Although bees may in fact be useful to other species, in no sense are we justified in saying that the motives of bees are altruistic.

Yet Paley (like Ray) saw all natural wonders as examples

of God's design. Charles Darwin (1809–1882), who was intimately acquainted with Paley's writings, showed that the hypothesis of divine design was not necessary; to explain natural
adaptations we need assume nothing more than the necessities
for survival. In every species, at all times, there is much variability in structure and behavior, and some of the variability is
inheritable. (The modest assumption of "some" is all that is
needed to make the Darwinian scheme work.) Those individuals who might altruistically devote some of their time to caring for other species without getting something in return would
necessarily devote less time to taking care of members of their
own species (especially their own children). More egoistically
oriented individuals devoting less time to the care of other
species, should—on the average—leave more offspring behind.
Such differential survival, continued generation after generation, will purify a species of altruism toward other species. That
is the way natural selection works.

The evidence for Darwin's natural selection is now overwhelming. At the logical level the idea is as close as we can get
to a truth that is self-evident. Variants that survive in greater
numbers become predominant. How could it be otherwise?
How could adaptations that resulted in fewer surviving offspring become the dominant forms? Egoism is easy to understand; altruism is a puzzle.

As far as between-species altruism is concerned we can forget
the puzzle: it does not exist. (Symbiotic mutualism between
species exists—but that is no problem. Both species benefit; it is
not altruism.) But within a single species altruism, or something very much like it, can be found.

Many different relationships are possible among individuals
of the same species. To make sure that we do not lose sight of
any of the possibilities I have listed them in Table 1. What is
there called the protagonist is simply "the party of the first

TABLE 1
Effect of Intraspecific Actions on Reproductive Success

Popular names of the actions are given in the boxes. Possible persistent relations are shown in unshaded boxes; less common, nonpersistent, or "marginal" actions are shown in shaded boxes.

		Antagonist Effect of protagonist's actions on the reproductive success of the antagonist		
		Gain	Loss	Neutral
Protagonist Effect of protagonist's actions on his own reproductive success	Gain	1 Cooperative	2 Selfish or Sadistic	3 Egoistic
	Loss	4 Altruistic or Masochistic	5 Spiteful or Sado-masochistic	6 Masochistic
	Neutral	7 Altruistic or Benevolent	8 Sadistic	9 Pointless

part," the antagonist being "the party of the second part." The adjectives in the boxes are ones commonly used in speaking of human activities; they are oriented from the point of view of the protagonist. An action may produce a gain or a loss in an individual's reproductive performance; or the result may be neutral. Similarly with respect to the antagonist. That makes $3 \times 3 = 9$ possibilities.

Practically speaking, we can ignore actions that are neutral with respect to either member. It is reasonable to assume that the protagonist must act somewhat as an economizer who will not habitually waste his time on neutral actions; and that it is unlikely that any action is completely neutral for the antagonist. Because such possibilities will not be discussed further, five boxes are shaded in the figure; I have, however, left them in the array on the chance that their presence may suggest something to the reader that I have overlooked.

The terms in the table that most need discussion are *masochistic, sadistic,* and their hybrid, *sado-masochistic.* Originally these words had an exclusively sexual reference, but time has broadened their meaning. It is the broader sense that is meant here. The word *sadism* is derived, of course, from the Marquis de Sade (1740–1814), who "got his jollies" from torturing other people. *Masochism* comes from the name of an Austrian writer, Leopold von Sacher-Masoch (1836–1895), whose novels depict the pleasure a person gets by making *himself* miserable. From a simple-minded, rationalistic standpoint both forms of punishing behavior present something of a puzzle. How can it possibly benefit me to cause pain to others? Even more pointedly, what do I gain by causing pain to myself? We are tempted to call both sadism and masochism "unnatural," and so in a sense they are. But they exist. De Sade existed, and so do people of the sort Sacher-Masoch described. In trying to account for such behavior psychiatrists have evolved the concept of "secondary gains," which raises interesting problems in the methodology of science. This area of study is fascinating and important, but it is a bit to one side of our present interest.

The important point is that within a species something that looks like altruism exists: box 4 in Table 1 has members. Only in the past generation has a rigorous biological basis for altruism been worked out. The biological explanation is precise though somewhat restricted. After learning what it amounts to we will try to see if it can be broadened.

The willingness of animal parents to sacrifice themselves for their young is legendary. The athletic performance of spawning salmon swimming up torrents is followed by the death of the parents after the eggs are laid; a ground-nesting bird feigns injury and risks capture as she leads a potential predator away from the nest; and a male spider, in mating and thereby insuring that he has offspring, risks being eaten by the female. One can even argue that the extra nourishment the male spider unwillingly furnishes his mate makes her a better mother.

Richard Alexander has described a most fascinating example

of parental altruism in one species of crickets (Gryllidae).[2] A mother of the species *Anurogryllus muticus* allows herself to be eaten by her own offspring, thus giving them a better start in life. Greater love hath no woman than this! No doubt any genes for lesser altruism in this species are strongly selected against. Vacuous though the speculation may be, one cannot but wonder what is in the mind of the normal *Anurogryllus* mother as she offers herself up to her children. If there were cricket psychiatrists, would they not detect a bit of masochism in the psychology of these mothers? If so, they would no doubt call it *gryllusism*, a term that would be as laudatory among crickets as *Americanism* is among Americans. In fact, I think Freud would have loved the story of the crickets had he known of it, and he might well have coined the term *gryllusism* to stand in place of *masochism*. The explanation of this term would be richer and more meaningful than the one we are stuck with.

There is a serious point to this whimsy: it has to do with terminology. Box 4 contains two terms, "altruism" and "masochism." We could also include "nobly sacrificial." All three labels have reference to the same objectively determinable facts; as a physicist would say, they have the same dimensions. Which term one uses is determined by one's intentions toward the reader—by the way one wants to structure his perception of reality. (Language serves two functions: to facilitate thought, and to prevent it.) It would be desirable to have a term that is exclusively descriptive without implying anything about motives. "Protagonist–loss, antagonist–gain behavior" would do, and it yields the convenient acronym "PLAG behavior"—but I'm afraid we already have too much jargon for this to catch on. We will just have to make do with a popular term, to which we can append a footnote (and hope that it does not drop off). I favor "altruism" as the popular term least contaminated by hypothetical motivation, trustingly adding the footnote, "I really mean PLAG behavior."

In this sense, does altruistic behavior exist among nonhuman animals? Harry Power has thrown light on this problem with some simple experiments using mountain bluebirds.[3] As is true among many bird species, when one member of a mated pair disappears (e.g., by an act of predation) its place is usually soon filled by a new partner from the surrounding reservoir of the unmated. If this replacement occurs when there are nestlings will the new consort take care of young not its own? (We must use the word *consort* rather than *mate* because birds are physiologically programmed not to mate sexually while there are young underfoot.) By kidnapping one or the other of the parents Power created ten such consort pairs.

A male parent feeds the young, cleans the nest, and gives warning calls when the nest seems threatened. Of the eight consort males observed, not one behaved in any of these ways toward nestlings not his own. Of the two female consorts one did care for the nestlings—but only after an interval of five days of non-care. Power argued that it was reasonable to regard this single instance as a reproductive error rather than as a case of genuine altruism.

The numbers are small, so the evidence might be dismissed were it not for the fact that everything we know about step-parentage among animals fits into the same pattern. A conquering lion kills the young of his vanquished predecessor;[4] so do langur males.[5] In mice, a similar result is brought about less violently by the Bruce effect: the mere odor of a new male causes a pregnant female to abort, thus making herself ready for impregnation by her new mate.[6]

All this is easily explained on a strictly Darwinian basis. One of the most serious misunderstandings of Darwin's theory is the belief that natural selection works for the good of the species. Not so: natural selection benefits individual germ lines, a process that may or may not benefit the species. (We will return to this important matter in chap. 6.) From the point of view of the species the Bruce effect introduces inefficiency into the reproductive process; but from the point of view of the germ line of the interloping male mouse the Bruce effect is efficient. It increases the number of his offspring by reducing the total number of offspring for the species. The benefit of the Bruce effect from the female's point of view is that it avoids wasting the time and effort of carrying a pregnancy to term only to have the resulting offspring killed by a male interloper (as would presumably happen).

Adult behavior that favors the survival of children in general —any children—could be regarded as altruistic: it is very rare. Behavior that favors one's own children only, if it is to be called altruism at all, must be called by a special name: *kin altruism*. The selective value of kin altruism is easy to understand.

Kin altruism is obviously not "pure" altruism. The child that a parent makes sacrifices for is, in part, the parent himself. To be specific, one-half of the child's genes are the same as those of any one parent. In sacrificing himself for his child a parent is, as it were, demi-selfish. If a demi-selfish parent leaves more offspring than a fully selfish one then demi-selfishness will be selected for as against pure selfishness. Behavior that is demi-selfish might just as well be called demi-altruistic. Genetically based fractional altruism is easier to understand than pure altruism.

Darwin grasped the basic idea of kin altruism, but it was another century before its significance was fully appreciated. William D. Hamilton, who coined the term kin altruism, is principally responsible for the theory.[7] He has shown how altruism in the animal kingdom is related to the degree of kinship of the actors (Table 2). The loss the protagonist suffers need not be so extreme as loss of life but it is easier to see the structure of the theory if we consider only this extreme case.

Suppose an individual sacrifices his life to save the life of his blood brother. If this behavior is in part due to genes, will natural selection favor it? The answer is no, because on the average the brother saved has only half the genes of the brother who, together with his genes, is lost. But if this type of behavior led, on the average, to the saving of two brothers in each generation it would be neutral in value. Two is the break-even number for altruism among brothers. If three were saved altruism would be favored by natural selection.

The break-even point is the reciprocal of the degree of genetic kinship. An altruist would have to save the life of more than eight of his cousins before such behavior could be selected for at that degree of kinship. When the degree of relationship is so slight as to be nearly zero, the break-even point is nearly infinity (see next to last line of Table 2). That would be an instance of nearly pure altruism; on a simple Darwinian basis it is all but impossible. (When the relationship is really zero, as it is between members of different species, it cannot be said that there is any break-even point. The more members of another species saved, in an act of pure altruism, the less space there is in a finite world for the savior and his relatives.)

What all this amounts to, of course, is a quantification of the old saw, "Blood is thicker than water." To the extent that behavior is genetically determined we would expect to observe altruistic behavior more often among siblings than among cousins. This statement does not preclude other explanations of such behavior. The relative importance of each partial explanation must be determined in each particular instance.

Does non-kin altruism also exist? Robert Trivers has proposed a term that throws light on the problem: *reciprocal altruism*.[8] Patterns of helping behavior between unrelated members

TABLE 2

Quantitative Basis of Kin Altruism

When self is completely sacrificed (as by death), if sacrificing behavior is to be of selective value the number of others it saves of the relationship specified must be just greater than the break-even point number. Incomplete sacrifice follows the same quantitative rule.

Relationship	Genetic kinship	Break-even point
Self; identical twins; members of same clone	1	1
Parent and child; full sibs	½	2
Grandparent and child; half sibs; uncle and nephew; aunt and niece; double first cousins	¼	4
First cousins	⅛	8
"Unrelated" members of the same species	nearly 0	nearly ∞
Members of different species	0	nonexistent

can be selected for if the two actors of a pair take turns being benefactor and beneficiary; provided that either member will break off the relationship if the other persistently refuses to take his turn being benefactor; and provided further that the members of such a reciprocating couple will prosper more than individuals not acting together in this way.

In other words, "You scratch my back and I'll scratch yours." Trivers has shown how such behavior can be selected for when behavior is largely determined by heredity, as it is in many animals. But reciprocal aid is of value even when the hereditary component is negligible. In the human realm we do not speak of reciprocal altruism but of the principle of the *quid pro quo*, which governs the everyday exchanges between human beings that we feel do not qualify as altruism. Speaking carelessly we might say that a peasant "gives" the doctor a suckling pig and the doctor "gives" the peasant a pill, but these are not really gifts. What is involved is a trade, a quid being exchanged for a quo. This is not pure altruism (which is what "gives" suggests) but reciprocal altruism. Because of the relative incommensurability of such natural units as chickens, pigs, houses, and personal services, barter is technically complicated.

It was a great moment in the progress of humankind when money was invented. Money, as Edward O. Wilson has observed, is "only a quantification of reciprocal altruism."[9] It has, as is well known, additional advantages over barter. Money, unlike vegetables, is not perishable and can be stored; thus the quid can be separated from the quo in time without depending on people's untrustworthy memories. Free-floating demands on unnamed persons for unnamed services does away with much of the emotional aura of barter—an advance about which there are mixed feelings. Anyone who has observed bartering taking place in a primitive society is struck by the richness of the human experience. But it does take up a lot of time.

One can argue that the term *reciprocal altruism* is a misnomer because each participant in a barter is really trying to secure the most favorable rate of exchange for himself. *Coupled egoism* might be a better term. Down through the centuries, many derogatory remarks have been made about money, but the quantitative explicitness of the quids and the quos that money makes possible allows coupled egoism to approach more closely a true state of reciprocal altruism. Biological heredity makes kin altruism possible; the social invention of money makes possible a more widespread and more flexible reciprocal altruism between unrelated members of the species.

The world of human interchanges is immensely more complicated than that of animal interactions. The presumption of egoism can certainly explain most human behavior, but can it explain all? Suppose I willingly make a material sacrifice for you, and all that you give me in exchange is a pretty smile. Shall we say that I am an altruist because—on the material level—your gain is my loss? Or, if I admit that my psychological gain from observing your pleasure is greater than my material loss, are we to call me an egoist? Logically, the issue is undecidable; yet the alternative explanations are biologically reconcilable. For many species sociality has selective value, and, God knows, we are social. For a social animal, merely observing the pleasure of others is a reward. Measuring psychological gains against material losses is certainly a difficult problem, but millions of years of evolution have selected us to do just that. We may not do it very well, and we may not be very consistent, but we manage somehow.

With respect to the language they prefer for describing the phenomenon, people fall into two camps: those who call behavior of the sort just described egoistic and those who do not. Those who reach the egoistic position from an initial belief in altruism are often embittered by their disillusionment. The French mystic Fenelon (1651–1715) suffered from the change. "All generosity, all natural affection," he wrote to Madame de Maintenon, the wife of Louis XIV, "is only self-love of a specially subtle, delusive and diabolical quality."[10] A biologist can agree with everything but the flavor of this judgment: why should we call self-love channeled into the service of others "diabolical"? Only crippling illusions about human nature can explain this choice of adjective.

The repertoire of psychological rewards is significantly influenced by the organization of society. The English jurist Henry Maine (1822–1888) divided societies into two classes: status societies and contract societies. The former survive more readily under conditions of low population density, low worker mobility, and high social stability. Circular causation enters in.

What the individual can do is determined largely by who he is (i.e., by his status), and he finds significant psychological rewards in fulfilling his status well. In contrast, rapid social change, high worker mobility, and large populations all tend to shift society over to a contract basis, with its explicit rewards, its explicit quid pro quos. The terms of a contract are negotiable; status is not. Most societies are mixtures of the two polar types. It is understandable that the people whose status entitles them to large rewards tend to magnify the advantages of a status society, while those whose rewards are less seek the advantages of contracts—and want to renegotiate them. Members of the first group are generally called "conservatives." It is amusing to note that a famous status-glorifying hymn by Cecil Frances Alexander (1818–1895), "All Things Bright and Beautiful," was written in the same year as the *Communist Manifesto*, namely 1848:

> The rich man in his castle,
> The poor man at his gate,
> God made them, high or lowly,
> And ordered their estate.

This sentiment is a far cry from the temper of our time; it seems also to diverge from the trend. Yet, for all that can be said against a status society—and there is much—there is also something to be said for it. So much time and attention in a contract society are devoted to negotiating and renegotiating the quid pro quos that there are inevitably moments in the lives of all of us when we grow weary of quid counting. Like Wordsworth, we impatiently protest

> Give all thou canst, high Heaven rejects the lore
> Of nicely calculated less or more....[11]

This yearning for a world of uncalculated giving is nowhere shown more clearly than in a remarkable book published in this decade, *The Gift Relationship* by Richard Titmuss.[12] The author has two axes to grind: a particular one, and a more general one for which the particular is merely illustrative. His particular concern is the safety of the blood donor system. In England it is an entirely voluntary system; in the United States we use both paid donors and volunteers. Because many of the paid donors are Bowery bums in poor health, transfusion often produces hepatitis. This danger is greater in the United States than it is in England. Titmuss regards a paid system as inherently more dangerous and less reliable than a volunteer system. His reasons for thinking so are unconvincing, as has been shown by Kenneth Arrow.[13]

Titmuss's more general thesis bears on the present problem. He characterizes his major point in these words: "This study ... is ... concerned with the values we accord to people for what they give to strangers; not what they get out of society."[14] Remarkably, he asserts that a mixed system of volunteer and paid donors is impossible or unacceptable, because "to abolish the moral choice of giving to strangers could lead to an ideology to end all ideologies."[15]

> If the opportunity to behave altruistically—to exercise a moral choice to give in non-monetary forms to strangers—is an essential human right then this book is about the definition of freedom. Should men be free to sell their blood? Or should this freedom be curtailed to allow them to give or not to give blood? And if this freedom is to be paramount do we not then have to regard social policy institutions as agents of altruistic opportunities and, thus, as generators of moral conflict and not simply as utilitarian instruments of welfare?[16]

If this passage is not enough, the entire book suffices to show that the author's questions are rhetorical. He clearly yearns for a world in which social institutions *generate* moral conflict. To a scientist, this attitude sounds painfully familiar. Just as language is often used as a way of preventing thought, so also may research and scholarly investigation be used to generate problems rather than solve them. Cyrus Levinthal has commented on this failing among biologists.[17] The psychiatrist Lawrence Kubie has, on the basis of more extensive experience, remarked: "I have known scientists of great ability whose work nevertheless always tended to be vague and ambiguous. Some of these men unconsciously designed their laborious experiments so as to prove nothing."[18] Such an investigator, Kubie says, "uses scientific research precisely as the man with a handwashing compulsion uses soap and water, or as an addict uses drugs."[19]

As a biologist with a strong interest in ethical matters I find this insight a valuable tool in evaluating the works of professional ethicists. If one is not to waste one's life chasing will-o-the-wisps a reader must, at the moment of first plunging into a new book, ask: "Is the author really trying to solve problems, or is he one of that large band who connive to create problems?" I do not know when I have found a writer who acknowledges as openly as Titmuss does his desire to create a world that will generate more moral conflict. I don't think we are being overly severe if we call scholars like Titmuss "ethical anarchists."

The intensity of his yearning is painfully obvious in his panegyric of "the free gift of blood to unnamed strangers," in which gift, he says,

> there is no formal contract, no legal bond, no situation of power, domination, constraint or compulsion, no sense of shame or guilt, no gratitude imperative, no need for penitence, no money and no explicit guarantee of or wish for a reward or a return gift. [All such gifts] are acts of free will; of the exercise of choice; of conscience without shame.[20]

We have now reached a point at which theory can be tested against observation. Titmuss's theory is that pure altruism is both possible and productive of desirable effects; and that it does not require the spur of constraint, compulsion, shame, guilt, or the hope of reward. What does the literature of anthropology have to say about this? Alas for Titmuss, it is uniformly discouraging. To cite but one study among scores, George Foster's book about a primitive Mexican community in Tzintzuntzan[21] should convince anyone of the destructive effect on human amiability of substituting implicit and ambiguous voluntarism for explicit contract. A careful reading of the classic study *The Gift* by Marcel Mauss[22] leads to a similar conclusion. Everyone knows about the pathology of the anti-economic altruism embodied in the potlatch of the Northwest Indians. Replacing the explicitness of written sanctions (laws), money, and recorded debts with the ambiguity of pseudovoluntary gifts (as Titmuss would have us do) would greatly magnify the power and destructiveness of envy.[23]

Titmuss embraces the idea of the uncoerced gift as a way of increasing human freedom. But all that we know about non-market economies shows that people living in such societies enjoy less psychological freedom in their functions than we do. At best, the ambiguous and nonexplicit system of unpriced gift-exchanges requires that the practitioners devote an unconscionable amount of time to calculating Who's ahead? and Who owes whom what? The negotiated and explicit quid pro quo frees people to devote more time to looking for values greater than the values of exchange. Money can make people less materialistic.

The sad and curious fact is that Titmuss, at one mental level, "knows" that the historical record gives his theory little support. In a passage that precedes the one given above he says:

Acts of giving are, in many societies, a group affair, woven into the fabric of being, and take place in personal face-to-face situations. . . . More significant is the reality of the obligation or compulsion to give. In all that Mauss, Lévi-Strauss, Homans, Schwartz and others have written on gift-exchange there emerges a vivid sense of the immense pervasiveness of the social obligation—the group compulsions—to give and to repay, and the strength of the supporting sanctions: dishonour, shame and guilt.

Every gift-exchange dyad in such societies—and maybe, in some sense in our own societies—is thus characterized by elements of moral enforcement.[24]

Then coming back to his ideal of a purely voluntary scheme of blood donation, Titmuss admits that:

No donor type can, of course, be said to be characterized by complete, disinterested, spontaneous altruism. There must be some sense of obligation, approval and interest; some awareness of need and of the purposes of the blood gift; perhaps some organized group rivalry in generosity.[25]

In the light of this damaging admission, how is it possible for the author to support his scheme of pure voluntarism as the true path to that illusive good we call freedom? Apparently because he sees the corruption of traditional gift relationships as a consequence of the fact that they are not disinterested because the participants to the exchange know each other and invidiously keep score. To get rid of envy and all its horrid progeny, says Titmuss, we need only expunge the personal element from the system by giving only to strangers: then the giving will be truly disinterested.

This hypothesis is most remarkable. It is so remarkable that, if true, the author surely deserves the Nobel Peace Prize. The question is, is it true? Or, to put the matter more favorably, in what sort of society might it be true that people would prefer giving to strangers over giving to relatives and friends?

In a poor society? Certainly not. The literature on this point is absolutely consistent. For the chilling effect of poverty on disinterested action in India read *Behind Mud Walls*[26] or *The Autobiography of an Unknown Indian.*[27] That the situation is no better among the poor of Italy is amply attested to by Banfield's *The Moral Basis of a Backward Society.*[28] As Leonard Covello says, "It is impossible to imagine the *contadino* [peasant] in South Italy contributing to the Red Cross."[29] In a poor society even those who could afford to be altruistic are unlikely to be so: "When members of the upper class are asked who is known as particularly public spirited . . . some find the idea of public-spiritedness unintelligible."[30]

But perhaps poverty is not the essential cause of the nearly pure spirit of egoism shown in such cultures? (At their most expansive, such people muster the virtue Banfield calls "amoral familism.") Would we fortunate few who are the fullest inheritors of "the great tradition" of Western civilization behave differently under conditions of penury? Documents bearing on the case are absolutely consistent and conclusive: *we* are no better than anyone else. The relevant literature is that of behavior in the prison camps of the Second World War. Langdon Gilkey's account of the *Shantung Compound* (in which he was incarcerated) is one of the best. Under the stress of need, altruism shrank almost to the vanishing point as egoism took over. There were some differences among individuals, of course, but they were less differences in behavior than differences in language. Gilkey, himself a minister, reserved some of his harshest comments for the theologically trained missionaries of the camp, who showed themselves extremely adept at perceiving the will of God in their wholly egoistic actions. As Gilkey put it: "Teaching high ideals to men will not in itself produce better men and women. It may merely provide the taught with new ways of justifying their devotion to their own security."[31]

One more possibility of saving Titmuss's theory remains.

What about altruism in a prosperous society? Can unstructured voluntarism be substituted for institutional coercion and the incentives of the marketplace in a really rich society? Here Titmuss is on better ground: after all, we do support the Red Cross, which the peasants of South Italy do not. But I do not think Titmuss's theory can be saved even here. A very simple thought experiment should settle the question.

We now use coercion to collect the federal income tax. If Titmuss is right we should be able to do away with coercion, calling on people to volunteer what they regard as their rightful taxes. Freely responding to this call taxpayers would be giving to "the stranger"—i.e., to the national government and all the other citizens it serves. According to Titmuss, such disinterested and altruistic behavior should make people feel marvelously free. Moreover, Titmuss should be delighted with the way this opportunity would generate the moral conflicts he would like to see increase in number and intensity. (It just might generate conflicts of other sorts as well.)

I have spent a great deal of time on Titmuss's book for several reasons. It deals with an important subject; it has been reviewed unusually widely; and its novel sentiments have been much praised. The author's view of human nature is not a peculiar one; on the contrary, it is close to becoming fashionable, and therein lies the danger. Reconstructing society in all departments (far beyond the realm of blood donation), as Titmuss urges us to do, on a basis of pure altruism—and it is only *pure* altruism that Titmuss recommends—would, if my perception is correct, utterly destroy the delight in giving that the author seeks to encourage. This is no light condemnation, but I see no escape from it. It is based on more than theoretical predictions: experience confirms it. Mauss's study of status societies identifies the hypocrisy of gift-giving in no uncertain terms. He says that gifts in an archaic society are in theory voluntary, disinterested and spontaneous, but [they] are in fact obligatory and interested. The form usually taken is that of the gift generously offered; but the accompanying behavior is formal pretence and social deception, while the transaction itself is based on obligation and economic self-interest.[32]

It is curious that Titmus could cite Mauss so frequently with so little evidence that he had read him.

How can anyone be so mistaken about the nature of the gift relationship? I think the answer is quite simple. The origins of the error reach back into our earliest childhood. A story from the family of Sigmund Freud lays bare the roots. Freud's children, like many others, were shielded from knowledge of money matters beyond their own small allowances. As a result they had a poor appreciation of the quid pro quos that keep the wheels of the social order turning. His eldest daughter once

saw her aunt paying money to a servant and asked her what it was for. On being told it was wages, she vehemently asserted that her mother did nothing of the sort; their servants, and above all her Nannie, worked purely for love. When she was contradicted and told the truth she broke into tears and wept the whole night through.[33]

Parent–child exchanges, like all exchanges, observe the rule of quid pro quo, but the nature of the exchange is often not obvious. What the child gives the parent is particularly subtle: in the present, delight; for the future, hope—nothing so blatant as bottles of milk and clean diapers. To the parents this is obvious. But in the beginning at least the child supposes the relationship to be one of pure altruism, in which the child is an untaxed beneficiary. Parents—or those in parental positions (Nannies)—seem to the child to be all-giving. What the child is compelled to do (e.g., wash his hands) is not viewed as part of an exchange.

The process of growing up is in part a process of gradually becoming aware of the quid pro quos of the world—the obvious ones first, the less obvious ones later. Different people grow up at different speeds. Some seem hardly to mature at all; some of the cleverest of these write books on ethics.

The little Freud girl, like most children during part of their lives, thought her happiness depended on being loved "for herself alone," not for something she (or her guardians) exchanged with those who gave love to her. The yearning for unqualified love has been neatly dealt with in Yeats's poem "For Ann Gregory," a dialogue between a pretty young girl and someone of more mature years. First the older person speaks:

> "Never shall a young man,
> Thrown into despair
> By those great honey-coloured
> Ramparts at your ear,
> Love you for yourself alone
> And not your yellow hair."

> "But I can get a hair-dye
> And set such colour there,
> Brown, or black, or carrot,
> That young men in despair
> May love me for myself alone
> And not my yellow hair."

> "I heard an old religious man
> But yesternight declare
> That he had found a text to prove
> That only God, my dear,
> Could love you for yourself alone
> And not your yellow hair."*

---

*From *The Collected Poems of W. B. Yeats*, copyright 1933 by Macmillan Publishing Co., renewed 1961 by Bertha Georgie Yeats. Reprinted by permission of Macmillan Publishing Co. (New York), M. B. Yeats, Miss Anne Yeats, and the Macmillan Co. of London and Basingstoke.

The yearning to be loved "for one's self alone" is perfectly normal, but it is unwise to fashion one's expectations by this yearning once the years of childhood are past. As we grow older and move in larger, more impersonal circles we realize that we must give as well as get. Being attractive or charming or pleasant is a form of giving.

Who speaks for altruism? In searching for the springs of human action, what people say about altruism must be seasoned with whatever knowledge we have of who says it and why. When someone urges that we can, or should, make altruism our guide we will be well advised to wonder why he says this.

If the speaker, like the poet's girl with the yellow hair, asks for altruism directed toward himself we have no great trouble deducing his motive: it is simple egoism. The strength of this impulse in the young is no secret, though it is also stronger among the old than we like to admit. The principal difference is in the way in which the young more openly express their expectation of altruistic help from others.

If the speaker praises altruism because that is the path he proposes to follow himself we should have no quarrel with him. His is the altruism he recommends; the rest of the world will benefit; and the altruist himself may very well be happier than the general run of humanity.

But what are we to say if the speaker urges altruism on others *for others*? At first glance this recommendation would seem to be altruistic, but we know too much of psychoanalysis to trust facile first impressions. We know that in the unconscious mind there is pronominal confusion—that *I, you, we,* and *they* get all mixed up in the unconscious, together with their predicates. As imperatives crystallize out of this confusion into the conscious mind there is no telling what subject will be hooked up with what predicate. But we know that in matters tainted with taboo and social disapproval the hopes and fears of the ego are often projected onto other actors. The person who hates is likely to attribute hate to others, and so on. In the ordinary way of science we cannot prove the projections we detect in others; but in reaching everyday decisions about important matters we must not close our eyes to the possibility of projection.

One of the most reliable signs that projection is going on is the repetitive and excessive use of emotional appeals. Let us look once more at Titmuss's ringing appeal for altruistic actions, italicizing the significant repetitions:

> free gift . . . to unnamed strangers [with] *no* formal contract, *no* legal bond, *no* situation of power, domination, constraint or compulsion, *no* sense of shame or guilt, *no* gratitude imperative, *no* need for penitence, *no* money and *no* explicit guarantee of or a wish for a reward . . .

To the psychoanalytically tuned ear, this is a clear and poignant call for help. If we are compassionate we should be moved by it—but to do what? If we fail to perceive the projection process going on we may try to organize the world in ways that will be destructive of human aspirations.

Is pure altruism possible? Yes, of course it is—on a small scale, over the short term, in certain circumstances, and within small, intimate groups. In familylike groups one should be able to give with little thought "of nicely calculated less or more." But only the most naive hope to adhere to a noncalculating policy in a group that numbers in the thousands (or millions!), and in which many preexisting antagonisms are known and many more are suspected. Untested strangers are required to work successfully together for common goals. When both altruists and egoists are thrown together in large, impersonal groups the game favors the egoists. In large groups altruism has little chance to grow by an infective process; it is most likely to be nipped in the bud. It does not become part of a self-fulfilling prophecy; it is selected against. "How could it be otherwise?"

When those who have not appreciated the nature of large groups innocently call for "social policy institutions [to act] as agents of altruistic opportunities" they call for the impossible. In large groups social policy institutions necessarily must be guided by what I have called the Cardinal Rule of Policy: *Never ask a person to act against his own self-interest.* It is within the limitations of this rule that we must seek to create our future. What we seek is not the best of all conceivable worlds but the best of all possible worlds. In the intimacy of small groups altruism may be substantial and important; in large groups enlightened egoism is the most powerful motive. It is in fact the best motive that we can rely on.

2

Responsibility in Systems

THE WORLD IS FINITE. The demands put on it by all living organisms are potentially infinite; this is especially true of human demands, because we have come closer than any other species to eliminating death, without making the necessary corrective adjustment in births. Adjusting demand to supply may present no particular difficulties within the circle of a small number of people, such as a family; so long as there is intimacy informal means of mutual control may suffice, and altruism (or a reasonable facsimile thereof) helps. We may even be unaware of the means by which we achieve peace and a reasonably satisfactory distribution in a small group.

For a large group, however—and anything over a hundred is large—we must have a policy. *Policy*, I would remind you, is derived from Latin and Greek words for the city, the state, and citizenship. Policy is concerned with large numbers of people; therefore it must be based on an unwavering adherence to the Cardinal Rule: *Never ask a person to act against his own self-interest*. In the light of what we now know of biology, psychology, and environmental matters, what policy holds out the best hope for the survival of human beings under civilized conditions?

Homo sapiens stands in the presence of great environmental riches: how shall we distribute them? Directly to the individual, or through the mediation of a group? And how shall we manage them—individually, or as a group? That makes $2 \times 2 = 4$ possible ways to manage and distribute the goods of the environment. These four possibilities are shown in Table 3. Naming

TABLE 3

Distributional Systems for Utilizing the Environment
(in their pure forms)

Case	Utilization of the environment by:		Proceeds go to:		Name of system	Marginal utility of next unit utilized
	Individual	Group	Individual	Group		
I	✔		✔		Privatism	
II		✔		✔	Socialism	
III		✔	✔		Commonism (system of the commons)	
IV	✔			✔	Altruism	

the alternatives is a problem. We want to use names that require little explanation, but we must watch out for connotations acquired by words in the past. The word *communism*, for example, is hopelessly ambiguous; and *democracy* is claimed by an astonishing variety of nations.

More to the point, every existing political system can be viewed as a mixture of the four distributional systems shown here. The mixture varies widely. The best mixture depends on many conditions (including tradition) and is not our concern here. What we must inquire into are the properties, the tendencies, and the consequences of each distributional system.

In defining the systems a concrete situation will help. Imagine a pasture inhabited by cattle, which people wish to exploit for food. The first possibility is to divide up the pasture into separate fenced plots, one plot to a person: "private property." The cows on my land are mine and I can harvest them at whatever rate I choose. This system we call *privatism*.

In the second distributional system, land and cattle are community property. The group decides on the harvest; it may do so directly by a sort of town meeting, or indirectly through a manager appointed by the group. This we call *socialism*.

In the third system the pasture is common property, but each individual can utilize it to whatever extent he wishes. In one variant the individual can kill as many common property cattle as he wishes; buffalo were exploited in this way on the western plains of North America. In the other variant a man can pasture as many private-property cattle as he pleases, only the owner of each cow being privileged to kill it. This distributional system was followed for centuries in England in the management of village commons, on which villagers could, at will, pasture their animals. This is the system of the *unmanaged* commons, or more briefly, "the system of the commons." Still more briefly, fitting it in with the other names, it could be called *commonism*. Unfortunately this word is likely to be confused with the better-known term *communism*. The meanings are related, of course, but *communism* is, as we have said, ambiguous, whereas the meaning of the new word is given precisely by the check marks for case III of the table.

The fourth possibility is of course *altruism*: some kind-hearted person takes care of the animals and then distributes the harvest to others. This system is not often followed, nor does any political system stake its survival on it. We include this case in the table only for logical completeness.

Are the consequences of the four possible distributional systems significantly different? Yes, but their relative values depend significantly on whether the marginal utility of the next unit (e.g., the next cow) is positive or negative. To emphasize how much hinges on this one fact the last column has been left blank in Table 3; if we put pluses in this column the analysis goes one way; if minuses, another.

In Table 4 the operational definitions of the systems are omitted and merely their names are given; but the properties of each system are deduced from its operational characteristics,

TABLE 4

Pioneer Conditions

Consequences of the various distributional systems.

Name of system	Marginal utility of next unit utilized (1)	Gain to community from next unit (2)	Re: Decision maker		
			His direct gain (3)	His intrinsic responsibility (4)	His temptation to sabotage information (5)
Privatism	+	0	+	+	0
Socialism	+	+	0	0	+
Commonism (system of the commons)	+	0	+	0	0
Altruism	+	+	0	0	0

not from its name. Imagine first a world of practically unlimited environmental wealth, the sort of world open to some of our ancestors in pioneer times. When pioneer conditions existed each buffalo killed was so much more meat available; its value, its utility, can be indicated by pluses in column 1. Under privatism and commonism this gain would go to individuals as shown by the pluses in column 3. Under the other two systems the gain would go first to the group (column 2), from which it might be redistributed. Columns 4 and 5 have been shaded because they simply are not very important in this table. (They will be in the following table.) The only thing that matters is the way the pluses of column 1 are distributed into one or the other of columns 2 and 3.

As a matter of fact, none of the differences shown in Table 4 are terribly important; the table is displayed principally to remind us of the world we have lost, the world of the pioneer. Under pioneering conditions, when there is food for the taking, any of the four distributional systems will work well enough. It is doubtful, however, that an altruistic system would be set up; and socialism would be just too much bother. What remains, in most pioneer communities, is a mixture of privatism and commonism. The pioneer keeps his own milch cow and fences in his vegetable garden, but takes his rabbits and deer from the commons. Technical skills of all sorts are essential (hunting, fishing, gardening, carpentry, etc.) but not much is needed in such a community by way of managerial skills (for the management of other people). This is one reason many of us look back on the pioneer days with nostalgia, despite their physical harshness. But, as we shall see, we will pay dearly if we try to live in the world as it is now by a morality appropriate only to the pioneer condition.

Increase in population sooner or later changes the pluses in column 1 to minuses (see Table 5). This change is connected with the carrying capacity of the environment, which we can illustrate by reverting to our example of cattle in a commons. To say that "the carrying capacity of a pasture is 100 cattle" is to say this: that up to the number 100, adding one more cow to the pasture increases the yield; the marginal utility of the next unit is positive. But beyond 100, adding one more cow actually decreases the total yield. Food used in animal metabolism produces no harvestable product. With too little food, all the grass is used to keep the cows alive, none of it being converted to additional meat. When animals are sufficiently crowded they actually lose weight.

TABLE 5
Crowded Conditions

Consequences of the various distributional systems when
the environment is stressed beyond the carrying capacity.

Name of system	Marginal utility of next unit utilized (1)	Gain to community from next unit (2)	Re: Decision maker		
			His direct gain (3)	His intrinsic responsibility (4)	His temptation to sabotage information (5)
Privatism	−	−	−	+	0
Socialism	−	−	0	0	+
Commonism (system of the commons)	−	−	+	−	(?)
Altruism	−	−	0	0	(?)

"The Tragedy of the Commons"

The idea of carrying capacity involves time in a significant
way. Cattle normally eat sweet grass and leave what they regard as weeds relatively untouched. Such selectivity causes no
trouble under uncrowded conditions because the sweet grass
has plenty of time to grow again; but more vigorous grazing
tends to eliminate the sweet grass entirely. When the carrying
capacity is exceeded each succeeding year sees the weeds gain
in ascendency; after a few years there may be almost nothing
else. In addition, trampling of the ground by too many feet
causes loss of soil, particularly from steep slopes. Unfortunately
the degradative processes on an overgrazed pasture may not be
obvious. Just slightly exceeding the carrying capacity in one
year may yield an obvious short-term gain in harvest, with only
subtle indications of the long-term loss to come. "Practical
men," that is, men with 20–20 vision for the short term and
severe myopia for the long, have been destroying the garden

spots of the earth for thousands of years. George Perkins Marsh was the first scholar to recognize this; his *Man and Nature*[1] was published in 1864. It was almost a century before this topic was extensively dealt with again, this time in a volume entitled *Man's Role in Changing the Face of the Earth*,[2] a work by many scholars and dedicated to the memory of Marsh. Even today, two decades after this monumental volume was published, what proportion of the earth's population understands the immensely destructive power of man's everyday actions? I would be surprised if it is as great as one in a thousand. We have a long way to go before this knowledge significantly influences policy. We are shocked at a country that is 90 percent illiterate. Our rate of ecological illiteracy, which is at least as high, poses an even greater threat to the interests of posterity.

Before political changes can be made people need to understand that a different morality is called for once the carrying capacity of an environmental system is reached. If we set altruism aside as a marginal case, below the carrying capacity the other three distributive systems all work well enough. Once the carrying capacity is exceeded only two of them work. The third, the system of the commons, is absolutely and categorically intolerable. Table 5 shows why this is so.[3]

Before proceeding further we must agree on the meaning to be assigned to the word *responsibility*. The trickiness of this word is illustrated by a chapter from the last days of Watergate. At one point President Nixon said that he was fully responsible for the decisions that were made; a few days later he refused to give up certain key documents to congressional investigators, asserting that executive privilege excused him from all such accountability. He denied responsibility *to* someone, while asserting that he was responsible *for* what happened. He laid claim to power. In the unending barrage of assertions and counterassertions of responsibility we will do well to keep always in mind two simple definitions:

responsibility to = accountability
responsibility for = power

It is understandable that each of us, as an egoistic being, seeks to minimize his responsibility-to-ness and maximize his responsibility-for-ness. Nixon was being only human in pursuing this path.[4] To be responsible *for* is to possess power of some sort. For those high in the social hierarchy it is power to control others; for those of low position it is the power to feel guilty for what one cannot control. (This is the curious maneuver of the masochist.) A person with political power knows little of the mental experiences of the masochist, and seeks as much real power as he can get. His public pronouncements constantly play on the ambiguity of the word *responsibility*, as he seeks to create the impression among his constituents that he eagerly embraces accountability, all the while he endeavors to augment his power to act independently of other people. Such are the consequences of being ambitious and human.

Public policy, to be successful, must be tied to accountability. To help keep this in mind we would do well to adopt as our formal definition of responsibility the one given by Charles Frankel:

A decision is responsible when the man or group that makes it has to answer for it to those who are directly or indirectly affected by it.[5]

Committed to this definition let us set about evaluating the various distribution systems under conditions of scarcity (Table 5). Again, the fourth system, altruism, is of so little importance, politically speaking, that we will ignore it (hence the shading in the table). The other three are significantly different. Privatism, which works well under conditions of abundance (Table 4), also can work under conditions of scarcity (Table 5). If the owner of a fenced pasture loads it with too many cows the loss (column 2) from transgressing the carrying capacity devolves on *him* (column 3): since both "gains" have the same sign ($-$) he is intrinsically responsible ($+$ in column 4).

What about socialism? The manager of a socialized pasture loses very little directly by a bad decision, so it is appropriate to list his direct gain as zero (column 3). Consequently his intrinsic responsibility is also zero (column 4). This is unsatisfactory to the community, of course, which therefore engineers into the system some *contrived responsibility*: rewards for good management and penalties for poor. If the social engineering is good the contrived responsibility of a manager may be as good as the intrinsic responsibility of a private enterpriser.

Which system is better? It is impossible to say. The answer depends on many things not resolvable in a simple analysis: population size, geographical dispersion, traditions, cultural heterogeneity, etc. Either system *can* work. Each has its characteristic weaknesses. Privatism with its intrinsic responsibility may be fine for those fully *in* the system, but it can be hell for those outside it—who may start talking of "responsibility" of a different sort and seek to destroy the system that gives them so few benefits. Also there is the positive feedback of social power that pushes private enterprise in the direction of monopoly (which is why we have the Sherman Anti-Trust Act of 1890 and its many progeny).[6]

As for socialism, its Achilles' heel is the contrived responsibility it depends on. The controls a community of men can contrive to place on its managers, the managers—egoistic like all men, and strongly motivated to survive—may contrive to escape. The advantage of position gives managers first whack at the statistics, which they can alter or suppress to hide evidence of their incompetence. Note the plus in column 5 for socialism. Whatever a nation's nominal political system may be, its defense department is always necessarily and completely socialistic. In the name of "national security" a defense department can almost completely control the flow of information. We are therefore not surprised to note that great waste and inefficiency are typical of defense departments, even in times of peace. *Quis custodiet ipsos custodes?* (who shall watch the watchers themselves?) is the perpetual problem of all socialistic systems. We have not yet found a general and stable solution to this problem.

For all their faults, both privatism and socialism *can* work, more or less, under conditions of both abundance and scarcity. Not so with commonism. It is not often in human affairs that we can make a flat, unqualified statement, but in this case we can: For any group of more than a thousand members, under conditions of scarcity the system of the commons cannot possibly work. Why not?

Consider the classic commons, loaded with cattle. Once the carrying capacity is reached, a uniquely destructive process is set in train when any of the herdsmen contemplates increasing the size of his herd. I cannot do better than quote from my original statement of the problem:

> As a rational being each herdsman seeks to maximize his gain. Explicitly or implicitly, more or less consciously, he asks: "What is the utility to *me* of adding one more animal to my herd?" This utility has two components:
>
> 1. A positive component, which is a function of the increment of one animal. Since the herdsman receives all the proceeds from the sale of the additional animal, the positive utility is nearly +1.

2. A negative component, which is a function of the additional overgrazing created by one more animal. But since the effects of overgrazing are shared by all the herdsmen, the negative utility for any particular decision-making herdsman is only a fraction of -1.

Adding together the component partial utilities, the rational herdsman concludes that the only sensible course for him to pursue is to add another animal to his herd. And another; and another . . . But this is the conclusion reached by each and every rational herdsman sharing a commons. Each man is *locked in* to a system that compels him to increase his herd without limit . . . in a world that is limited. Ruin is the destination toward which all men rush, each pursuing his own best interest in a society that believes in the freedom of the commons. *Freedom in a commons brings ruin to all.*[7]

The analysis just given in almost intuitive terms has since been carried out more rigorously by others.[8] Alfred North Whitehead has defined tragedy as follows:

The essence of dramatic tragedy is not unhappiness. It resides in the solemnity of the remorseless working of things. . . . This inevitableness of destiny can only be illustrated in terms of human life by incidents which in fact involve unhappiness. For it is only by them that the futility of escape can be made evident in the drama.[9]

It is clear that the drama of the commons, if continued to the end, necessarily concludes in tragedy.

This fact is symbolized by the opposite signs on the third line in columns 2 and 3 of Table 5. None of the other systems suffer from this outright opposition of individual interest and community interest. Because of this opposition we must say that each decision maker in a commons "enjoys" a *negative* responsibility, operationally speaking (column 4). *He is paid to do the wrong thing.* He is paid only in the short run, it is true; but without extraordinary measures, it is the short-run payoff that determines most individual strategies in this competitive world. (We will return to this difficult problem in chap. 4.)

Moralists try to solve problems like this by denouncing "selfishness" and "greed"; but denunciation is seldom any good. These pejorative terms, at best, do little more than label the extreme of egoism, and we must not forget that we are descended from an unbroken line of egoistic ancestors. (Those who were too altruistic left no persistent line of descendants.) We may want to curb egoism, but we had better not try to destroy it entirely. It is still needed for the survival of the human species. We cannot imagine a time when it will not be.

Concern for the interests of the community is also good and necessary. Hence our dilemma. "The essentially tragic fact," as Hegel said, "is not so much the war of good with evil as it is the war of good with good."[10] It is for this reason that the approach of absolutist ethics is nonproductive.

Relativistic, or situation, ethics[11] assumes that the best answer changes as the situation changes. Commonism is an acceptable system—it may even be the best system—when there is a plus in column 1 of our table (Table 4, pioneer conditions); but commonism is the worst of all systems when column 1 is afflicted with a minus (Table 5, crowded conditions). The fundamental assertion of situation ethics is this: *The morality of an act is a function of the state of the system at the time the act is performed.* "Help yourself" may be a good rule at the frontier; it is devastating in a crowded city.

One point about Table 5 deserves brief comment: the question mark in column 5 for the system of the commons. One could argue that the individual helping himself in a commons has no reason to deny the fact, or to try to control the flow of information about his actions or their consequences. Yet the fact is that individuals enjoying the freedom of a commons are often less than candid. They often use deceptive words to support the continuance of the system itself, despite its long-term tragic consequences. Oceanic fisheries are still run on the system of the commons. When the world was less populous the "Help yourself" policy worked well enough. But no more. Since 1969 the worldwide harvest of fish has been declining[12] in spite of, and because of, more intensive fishing efforts, suggesting that the maximum sustainable yield of the oceans is less than what we are now taking out each year. Some species of whales and fish are near extinction. The tragic drama is inexorably continuing, in part because those who momentarily benefit by it deceive others (and perhaps themselves) by a rhetoric that extols "the freedom of the seas," a harvesting concept that was morally defensible earlier but is not so now.

What is to be done? Plainly it is counterproductive to seek to improve the technology of fishing, for every such improvement merely hastens the day of ruin. (Nevertheless, under the spur of competition such "improvements" will continue to be made.)

Should we appeal to people's conscience? This is a most tempting path to many people, but I have argued against it on compassionate grounds:[13]

> If we ask a man who is exploiting a commons to desist "in the name of conscience," what are we saying to him? What does he hear—not only at the moment but also in the wee small hours of the night when, half asleep, he remembers not merely the words we used but also the nonverbal communication cues we gave him unawares? Sooner or later, consciously or subconsciously, he senses that he has received two communications, and that they are contradictory:
>
> 1. (Intended communication) "If you don't do as we ask, we will openly condemn you for not acting like a responsible citizen."

2. (The unintended communication) "If you *do* behave as
we ask, we will secretly condemn you for a schlemiel, a
sucker, a sap, who can be shamed into standing aside
while the rest of us exploit the commons."

In a word, he is damned if he does and damned if he doesn't.
He is caught in what Gregory Bateson has called a "double
bind." Bateson and his co-workers have made a plausible
case for viewing the double bind as an important causative
factor in the genesis of schizophrenia.[14] The double bind may
not always be so damaging, but it always endangers the mental health of anyone to whom it is applied. "A bad conscience," said Nietzsche, "is a kind of illness."

. . .

Paul Goodman speaks from the modern point of view
when he says. "No good has ever come from feeling guilty,
neither intelligence, policy, nor compassion. The guilty do
not pay attention to the object but only to themselves, and
not even to their own interests, which might make sense, but
to their anxieties."[15]

We must, I think, suspect latent sadism in those who habitually try to control others by an appeal to conscience. This
appeal, so counterproductive among individuals, is even more
so among nations. The only nations that are substantially involved in whaling now are the USSR and Japan. For two decades there have been yearly attempts to get whaling nations to
agree voluntarily to reducing their catches to a level that might
eventually result in whaling for the maximum sustainable yield.
Since it is the system of the commons we are dealing with, appeals to voluntarism have failed. In desperation some environ-
mentalists have called for a boycott against Japan. Like most
such attempts this one has failed. (I cannot forget the bumper
sticker seen on a car in Los Angeles: "Boycott the Japanese:
Save the whales." The sticker was on a Datsun.) If a boycott
were successful it would probably provoke countermeasures on
the part of Japan—say purchasing soybeans from Brazil or lum-

ber from Norway instead of from the United States. It is hardly conceivable that Japan, keenly aware of her need for protein, would accept an effective boycott lying down.

The latest attempt to control whaling by nonsystematic means is that of the Greenpeace Foundation, which has sent out a crew on an 80-foot vessel to harass whalers on the high seas. We are told of idealists on board this vessel who appealed by megaphone to the captain of a Russian whaler to cease his activities in the interests of the whales and posterity. The captain's reply was, of course, of the sort that we of the older generation call "unprintable."[16]

And why should it not be? Whatever sneaking admiration we may have for the idealists of the Greenpeace Foundation— and I confess I have more than a little—their program is quixotic because it violates the Cardinal Rule by asking people to act against their own self-interest. The Swiss philosopher Helvetius (1715–1771) long ago saw the nature of the political problem:

> It is solely through good laws that one can form virtuous men. Thus the whole law of the legislator consists of forcing men, by the sentiment of self-love, to be always just to one another.[17]

We can put the matter this way. Adhering to the Cardinal Rule, we must never ask men to act as individual altruists; but we can appeal to them to adopt a sort of second-order altruism and act together to create laws that put an end to destructive modes of egoistic action. More exactly, if it can be demonstrated that the long-term effects of egoistic actions are deleterious we may be able to persuade people to forego short-term gains for the sake of the long term. How persuasive the case is depends significantly on quantities and the time scale. In any event, successful persuasion does not come easily. Most short-term beneficiaries of a going system view proposals of reform with a conservative and jaundiced eye, preferring, as Hamlet put it, to bear those ills they have than fly to others they know not of. Considering the uncertainty of technology assessment —and political organization is a sort of technology—this reluctance is understandable.

When a commons is involved such reluctance must not be allowed to persist unchallenged for long. To prevent the natural tragic end there is only one remedy in this ego-centered world: change the system. In the distribution of the wealth of the seas, which of the two other systems should we substitute for the commons? Considering the difficulties of fencing the ocean (as well as of "riding fence"), a socialistic system seems more logical, with an international body acting as custodians. Unfortunately this scheme runs up against the sanctified concept of traditional sovereignty, which views any dictation by an international body as an infringement on national sovereignty. What is needed is a willingness to regard national sovereignty as divisible. Logically it should be possible for a nation to insist on its right to place battleships in the open ocean and still accept restrictions on its right to put fishing fleets there. Many people have argued for such segmental limitation of national sovereignty[18]—so far without effect.

Converting parts of the seas to private property—really national property—is the other possibility. In spite of operational difficulties this alternative plan is making the better progress at the moment. More and more nations are unilaterally extending their right to exclusive control of fishing out to 200 miles from shore, with the passive acquiescence of other nations. For widely ranging marine species this limit is no solution, but it may help conserve inshore species. Extending sovereignty to 200 miles leads to some curious conflicts when islands under different jurisdictions are separated by a smaller distance, e.g., the Caribbean islands of Dominica (British) and Martinique (French), which are less than 30 miles apart.

Those who seek justice in the distribution of oceanic wealth are appalled to note that by the 200-mile rule Honduras would gain the right to another 126,000 square miles of ocean by virtue of her possession of the Swan Islands, which have a total population of 22 souls, whereas land-locked Upper Volta with its nearly six million people would have access to zero oceanic resources.[19] We may have to decide which we are more interested in: international justice now, or the conservation of oceanic resources for posterity. We may not be able to have both. In fact, we may not be able to have either. The act of moving from one system to another—from commonism, with its built-in appeal to our love of freedom, to either socialism or privatism—is something in the nature of a political miracle, a sort of lifting one's self by one's bootstraps. In the act of changing, people have to be persuaded or coerced to give up a system that furnishes obvious egoistic rewards (in the short run) for another whose rewards are principally long run.

One last warning: even when a national 200-mile limit is set, the danger of commonism is still not at an end. If a government allows its own nationals to treat the 200-mile strip as a commons, ruin is inevitable. Either national fisheries must be socialistically managed or the private enterprisers must be regulated by a bureaucracy. A closely regulated private enterprise system is operationally nearly identical with a socialistic system.[20] Both raise the vexing *Quis custodiet* problem.

Everyone carps at bureaucrats. A degradative process naturally causes regulatory agencies to become, in time, the prisoners of the people they are supposed to regulate. To play fast and loose with metaphors, one might say that watchdogs naturally evolve into kept women. The observed corruption of regulated systems may lead those whose patience is short to become anarchists or libertarians. Either response aggravates the conditions that provoke it. If there were any painless way of returning to a world in which resources greatly exceeded the demand on them —the world of the pioneer—we could then happily espouse the cause of greater liberty. But if we are unwilling or unable to escape a heavily populated world then we must, for almost all goods, abandon the commons as a distributive system and come to grips with the fiendish *Quis custodiet* problem. The difficulty of this question, no doubt, will discourage many; but ambitious young men and women who seek new worlds to conquer can hardly find a more fascinating or important problem. The quality of the future will be determined by our success in attacking it.

3

Ethical Implications
of Carrying Capacity

SELDOM IN HUMAN AFFAIRS does a massive governmental operation succeed better than its proposers dared dream, but the Marshall Plan did. The economy of Europe was reconstructed in a shorter time than had been thought possible. Of course the Europeans themselves were primarily responsible; but money from the United States played a crucial role.

While this effort was going on, the Luce journals (principally *Time* and *Life*) and Secretary of State John Foster Dulles were calling for a "new moral offensive"—but no one (not even they) quite knew what they meant. Then a minor worker in the State Department had an idea. His name was Ben Hardy. Why not extend the Marshall Plan to the world? Making no progress in State, he pulled strings and brought his idea to the attention of Harry Truman. The President liked it, and on 20 January 1949 he announced to the world that the United States "would accept the economic and social development of the underdeveloped territories on earth as a binding obligation." Thus was the modern institution of foreign aid born.[1]

It really is a new institution. Occasionally in the past Americans had sent food, clothing, or money to a stricken people, as we did to the Armenians in the 1920s; but the operation had always been a strictly temporary affair with most of the funds coming from private sources. The action was always a response to a crisis—military devastation, a volcanic eruption, an earthquake, or the like. What began in 1949 was an attempt to deal not with a crisis but with a crunch—with the chronic poverty that had afflicted two-thirds of the world for centuries. The missionary spirit that brought Christ to the heathen in the nineteenth century was reborn in the twentieth to bring prosperity to the poor. (Note that Secretary Dulles was a missionary child.)

From the first we had to wrestle with the problem of a label to attach to the objects of our charity. *Heathen* and *savages* were all right for the Victorians but not for us; even the accurate term *poor* would, we felt, hurt the feelings of the objects of our attentions. Since most of the rich and well-fed countries had a high degree of industrial development, the application of *post hoc* reasoning led to the conclusion that *development* = *prosperity*, so the poor countries were promptly labeled *undeveloped*. But before long everyone caught on to the fact that it was just a polite word for *poor*, so this term had to be abandoned. One face-saving euphemism after another had to be replaced as its "cover" was penetrated. The time-series ran: undeveloped → underdeveloped → developing → catch-up countries → emerging nations → Third World countries—"The Flight of the Euphemisms," we might call this ballet.[2]

In the late 1950s W. W. Rostow proposed a vivid image: the "takeoff point."[3] Each country's economy was like an airplane: all that was necessary to get it flying was to accelerate it ("develop" it) to the point where the economy could *take off* from the ground and then it was on its own. Foreign aid would thenceforth no longer be needed.

Alas! With few and arguable exceptions it has not worked

out that way.[4] The globalized Marshall Plan has not repeated the brilliant success of its progenitor. In addition to the substantial contributions of other countries, the United States itself spent $80 billion on genuine development aid (leaving out military aid that masqueraded as such). A quarter of a century and $80 billion later things are pretty much as they were—the gap between rich and poor countries is virtually unchanged. Why?

To begin with, there are many differences between postwar Europe and the poor world. Europe was faced with the job of *re*building a kind of civilization she had once known and was sure she could build again; but the poor were asked to create something utterly new in their experience. Europe's adult population is more than 98% literate; that of the poor countries is 2–30% literate. The philosophy of European people is Faustian–Promethean—"can do" and "let's try" are ingrained attitudes; traditionally poor people are essentially fatalistic. Europe's population had for a long time grown at less than one-half percent per year. Poor countries were growing faster than that; in most of them population increase soon approached three percent per year. The Marshall Plan was focused on about 100 million people; foreign aid had to deal with two billion—twenty times as many. The money allotted by the United States was about the same in the two programs—in the neighborhood of $3 billion per year. Even if the theory of the takeoff point is correct, so small an impetus to the ship of state might be only enough to make the crash at the end of the runway worse.

Many of us think the development theory of poverty is wrong. The technological image of the takeoff point is too mechanical. The phrase emphasizes speed only—as though poor countries and rich countries differed merely in some quantity measured along a single continuum. But the significant differences are categorical, cultural, fundamental. Psychologically the cultures of industrial and nonindustrial systems are worlds apart; you cannot get from one to the other just by going faster. The glib assumption that we can (and should) "make them just like us," which ruled the religious missionary efforts of the nineteenth century, rules the foreign aid missions of the twentieth.

A more fundamental approach to poverty is needed. All problems of fitting cultures to resources must be examined against the concept of the carrying capacity. Let us see first how it applies to other animals. That done we can then see what modifications need to be made in applying it to the human situation.

The disaster that develops when carrying capacity is ignored is marvelously clear in the population history of the reindeer on St. Matthew Island.[5] In 1944, 24 females and five males were turned loose on this island in the Bering Sea. Food was abundant, there were no predators, and hunting by man was negligible during the next twenty years. By 1957 the population had swelled to 1,350 reindeer; in the summer of 1963 it reached its peak of over 6,000 and then "crashed" during the winter when food was at its minimum. Three years later there were only 42 animals, all adults and all but one female. The future of the herd was in doubt.

A biologist studying the situation closely came to the conclusion that the carrying capacity of the environment was about five deer per square kilometer. That is, if the number never rose higher than this the herd could survive indefinitely—even through hard winters—in good health. In 1957 the island had only four deer per square kilometer, and they were 50 percent heavier than the animals on the mainland. The greater weight was no doubt accounted for by two factors: plenty of food, and lack of selective pressure against the fatter (and slower) animals by predators.

By 1963, the year of the crash, there were 18 animals per

square kilometer, and the average weight had dropped back to that of the mainland herds. In the process of crashing the island population virtually destroyed all the lichens on which reindeer depend.

This story is a highly abnormal one. Population crashes in nature are rare. Most of the time a population fluctuates within rather narrow limits. Figure 1 can stand as a generalization for

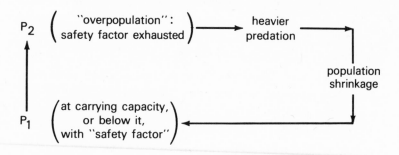

Figure 1. A population cycle with effective but not perfect control by predators. P_2 is greater than P_1. The more perfect the control the smaller the difference between P_2 and P_1.

most populations most of the time. The population level called P_1 is presumed to be at or near the carrying capacity. When the population rises much above it the excess provokes increased activity by the population-controlling factors—disease, predators, or (more rarely) starvation. The more severe control causes increased mortality, bringing the population back down near P_1, and the cycle starts over again. (If predators are involved they have their cycle too, which is much like that of the prey, but with a time-delay.) The principal difference between different populations is in the gap between P_1 and P_2. In finely adjusted natural systems the gap will be very small. Such stable systems are characteristic of complex tropical rain forests.[6] At the other extreme is the notorious example of the Arctic lemming, which lives in a relatively simple environment. The association of ecological complexity with population stability is thought to be an essential one, though the theory is in an unsatisfactory state.

The biological system on the 333 square kilometers of St. Matthew Island was obviously too simple: predators were missing. There was nothing to hold the population at or below the carrying capacity; consequently the reindeer population greatly overshot its proper level, overgrazed the plants and crashed, leaving the environment in shambles. The disaster could have been prevented by plugging suitable predators into the system —wolves, perhaps. More bluntly: by death. All organisms naturally and necessarily reproduce too much for their own good; for life to be sweet it must have death as a countervailing force.

Accepting the necessity of death even for wild animals comes hard for many people. The management of deer herds in the United States in the first half of the twentieth century was a disgrace. Because we would not accept and plan for timely deaths we caused many more deaths, which were untimely and more painful. The literature on which we have been raised glorifies the lamb and vilifies the wolf. We eliminated most of the predators in the United States and then wondered why our too-numerous deer showed signs of painful malnutrition. Our compassion for the "innocent" and helpless caused us to pass game laws that prohibited the shooting of does and fawns. Bucks, being males, were apparently not "innocent," though they were hardly any less helpless in front of a high-powered rifle. One buck suffices to fertilize many does, so population growth is affected very little when only bucks are shot.

By the late 1930s it was apparent to a few game managers what was wrong. The academic subject of game management was virtually created by Aldo Leopold (1887–1948), who began his life as an enthusiastic wolf hunter but changed his position

180 degrees when he realized that carrying capacity had to be the central concept in game management. It was not easy to reeducate a brainwashed public. A cruel blow to rational management was struck in 1942, when Walt Disney's *Bambi* was released. Many a biologist regards it as the most pornographic film ever put out. Its unqualified glorification of motherhood and babyhood and its vilification of hunters made the task of educating the public to the facts of life very difficult for a while.

The year after *Bambi* the state of Wisconsin, desperately trying to reduce its too-large and miserable deer population, authorized an open season on all deer. The resultant killing of 128,000 deer was not enough to solve the overpopulation problem but it was more than enough to evoke a public outcry against the measure. Leopold, as its principal architect, came in for particular attack. One of the arguments of his opponents is worth repeating for the light it throws on population problems.

Taking a census of wildlife is difficult, for obvious reasons. Sampling methods of uncertain reliability must be used. Leopold never tried to gloss over the unreliability of the game managers' estimates, because he knew it did not matter. His opponents did not understand that. When Leopold admitted that the estimate of 500,000 deer in Wisconsin before the 1943 deer-kill was a "pure guess" he was pilloried with these words:

> The infamous and bloody 1943 deer slaughter was sponsored by ... Mr. Aldo Leopold, who admitted in writing that the figures he used were PURE GUESSWORK. ... Imagine our fine deer herd shot to pieces by a man who rates himself as a Professor and used a GUESS instead of facts?[7]

The point, which the indignant critic did not understand, is that you do not have to count the deer to know if there is overpopulation. You should look at two things: the deer themselves (do they show signs of malnutrition?) and their environment (does it show signs of the degradation that follows from exceeding its carrying capacity?). Neither area nor population size need be known with any degree of accuracy: carrying capacity is the target we must keep our eye on as we look for the signs of exceeding it that are easy to read—once we know what to look for.[8]

It took twenty years for the Wisconsin public to get over the shock of the "massacre of '43" and be willing to examine the hunting problem rationally. Similar scenarios have been enacted in other states. The battle for rationality has to be fought state by state, county by county. It is a struggle to get people to see the centrality of the concept of carrying capacity.

Our primary concern here is with human populations, but before going on to these there are a few more principles we need to establish using nonhuman animals as exemplars.

First, it is ironically all too easy to get public support for measures that are counterproductive. In the dead of winter a report comes in of starving deer in the state parks. (Not so many would be starving, of course, if there were more predators.) Without thinking of the consequences, hunters and Bambi-lovers join hands and respond to the "emergency" in the same way: they pay to have bales of hay taken to the feeding grounds by truck or helicopter. Deer lives are saved, and the next spring the population begins its yearly growth from a higher level. This means that the next "emergency" will be greater and that meeting it with an input from an external food bank will bring the population—and the trouble—to a still higher level. The destructive system is diagrammed in Figure 2. Instead of a $P_1 \rightarrow P_2 \rightarrow P_1$ cycle, we have a $P_1 \rightarrow P_2 \rightarrow P_3 \rightarrow P_4 \ldots$ escalator, because of the inputs of food from outside the system. Or, to change the image, external inputs act like the

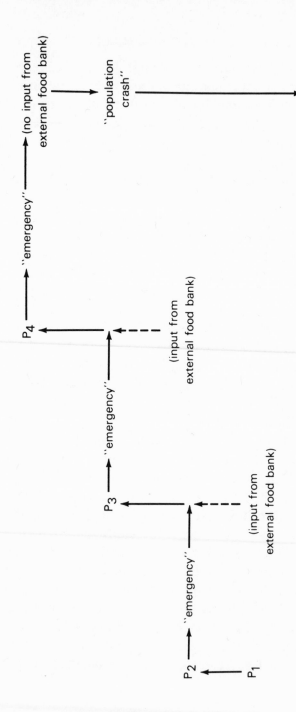

Figure 2. Escalation of emergencies by ill-advised input of food. P_{n+1} is greater than P_n. The input of food from outside the system acts like the pawl of a ratchet, preventing the normal adjustment downward.

pawl of a ratchet, keeping the population from dropping back to its original level. That might be all right if the world were infinite and if "philanthropic" inputs from outside the system could go on forever at ever higher levels. But they cannot. Some fine day philanthropy dries up, and the overexploited natural system (grass, lichens, or whatever) proves incapable of supporting the artificially large population. The crime of exceeding the carrying capacity is paid for with a population crash.

The same short-sighted "humanitarianism" that sponsors winter feeding also leads to killing predators and restricting hunting by human beings. Because hunters speak and vote, their cause is better presented than that of the nonhuman predators. That is a pity because natural predation is better for the well-being of a prey population than are human hunters. Natural predators are natural economists: they try to get their food with the least effort. Healthy prey animals in the prime of adulthood are difficult to catch, so predators focus most of their attention on the young, the old, and the sick.[9] What they leave is a herd in splendid average health—and not growing so rapidly. Human hunters, seeking handsome trophies, pursue a contrary policy. Population control by hunters is consequently qualitatively inferior to that by natural predators. Fortunately, the case for natural predators is now beginning to be heard. Books like Farley Mowat's *Never Cry Wolf*[10] are beginning to free the public mind from the stereotype of the Big Bad Wolf in "Little Red Riding Hood."

The struggle for rational game management has shown us that we must take a hard look at the "self-serving" argument. Most of the people who argued for extending the limits of legal hunting were themselves hunters. Opponents immediately denounced their argument as "self-serving": it was said that they wanted to change the rules just so they could shoot more deer.

In truth, the argument of the hunters *was* self-serving. The important policy question is this: was it also a good argument? In the interests of the herd, was there a need for killing more animals? Since the answer is yes, we reach an important general conclusion: *An argument that is self-serving may still be true.* The utility of identifying the self-serving character of an argument is that it puts us on the alert for prejudice and error. Any argument that is self-serving should be suspected, but it must not be dismissed out of hand. We must reason together.

One additional point needs to be made. If we extend the domain of ethics to include nonhuman animals, what is the ethics of killing deer? Should we follow the absolute rule "Thou shalt not kill"? Not if we have the well-being of the deer population in mind. Whenever the number of animals exceeds the carrying capacity of the environment by ever so little we should kill the excess as promptly as possible, before the stress of the excess degrades the environment and reduces its carrying capacity. As a matter of fact, prudence dictates that we apply control measures well before the carrying capacity is reached.

So long as the population is well below the carrying capacity there is no *need* to kill any of the animals. (There may be a *desire* to—on the part of some men—but that is another problem.) In other words, asked if the rule "Thou shalt not kill" is a good one we must answer, "It depends." Once we understand the ethical implications of carrying capacity we abandon ethical absolutism in favor of ethical relativism, or "situation ethics." The morality of an act, as we said before, depends on the state of the system at the time the act is performed.

It may be objected that we have merely replaced one absolute proscription ("Thou shalt not kill") by another ("Thou shalt not suffer the carrying capacity to be exceeded"). So we have; but we have not necessarily fallen into the absolutist trap. We recognize that the second directive may also be invalidated under some circumstances. I do not at the moment know what these might be, but an ethical situationist always tries to keep his mind open to the possibility of further changes in the moral directives he perforce has to adopt to give some stability to daily life.

Now we come to the human situation. Immediately the reader may bristle at his inference—it is certainly not my implication—that we must kill human beings whenever population exceeds carrying capacity. But, playing the role of both controllers and controlled, we human beings are unwilling to do so. We have good reasons for refusing, the validity of which I accept. *There is no need to kill*: we have better and more humane ways of achieving the same end, namely making population size match the carrying capacity. The question is, what are these better means? And how can we bring ourselves to use them?

Before proceeding with the inquiry we need to note one way in which the previous analysis is deficient for the human situation. The diagrams and the argument that accompanied them implicitly assumed that carrying capacity (ignoring fluctuations) is static. For most species most of the time, that is true. That was the assumption Malthus made when he wrote his *Essay on Population* in 1798. Unfortunately for Malthus's reputation, the carrying capacity of the earth for human beings has grown fantastically since his day. In part, it has increased because new lands have been opened up to human settlement (but this process is almost at an end). Even more important has been the growth of science and technology. Irrigation, fertilization, and new genetic strains of plants and animals have greatly increased productivity per hectare. So why worry? Can't this go on forever?

Marx's collaborator Friedrich Engels (1820–1895) said it could:

the productivity of the land can be infinitely increased by
the application of capital, labour and science.[11]

This sentiment, expressed in 1844, has been in the mainstream
of Communist doctrine down to the present time; it has also
been taken up by many non-Communists, e.g., promoters and
developers of large commercial enterprises, the more extreme
of the technological optimists and even a few of the older economists, now fortunately being displaced. Scientists almost
without exception disagree: they live in a world governed by
conservation principles, which have been called "impotence
principles" by the physicist Edmund Whittaker (1873–1956).
In the scientists' view, nothing is created. Matter is changed
from one form to another, and every change is paid for by the
loss of useful energy ("negative entropy"). To "create" one
thing is to have less of something else; and there is always a loss
of useful energy. And, as we have become particularly aware in
recent years, the creation of useful things is always accompanied
by the creation of noxious by-products—"pollution" we call
them—which take still more energy to process into less noxious
substances.

Living is an expensive game, and the greater the density of
population the more expensive it becomes. If we want reasonably pure air and pure water the carrying capacity of the earth
is much less than it is if we do not care what we breathe and
drink. More generally, for the human population, once it numbers in the hundreds of millions, what we call the carrying
capacity is inversely related to the material standard of living
we choose. He who says "The earth can support still more
people" is always right: for, until we reach absolute rock bot-
tom, we can always lower the standard of living another notch
and support a larger population. The question is, which do we
want: the maximum number of people at the minimum standard of living—or a smaller number at a comfortable, or even

gracious, standard of living? We are our own caretakers: the choice is ours.

We can choose not to choose, of course. Choosing and implementing the choice may be politically so difficult that we cannot, or will not, control our own future. In that case, humanity's population history will be not too different from that of uncontrolled animal populations: sooner or later there will be a dreadful population crash. If the human population of the world does suffer a general crash the result will be more dreadful than anything ever known for any other animal population. How so?

Harrison Brown, I believe, was the first person to appreciate the uniquely vulnerable situation of the most "advanced" of contemporary human societies.[12] In a book published a generation ago this geophysicist called attention to the significance of the progress of technology for the possibility of repeating this progress after a crash. The single substance copper can illustrate a large class of problems. Long before the invention of writing, men learned how to smelt copper and make tools and weapons from copper and bronze. Suppose our present civilization fell apart, as it might following an all-out nuclear war or a gigantic population crash: could we pick ourselves up and rebuild technological civilization as we know it? We probably could not.

Looking only at the copper component of the problem, we should note that preliterate man managed to create the Bronze Age only because of the ready availability of copper ores assaying greater than 20 percent; there was even some native copper from which to make the first copper tools around 8,000 B.C. Only the most primitive of means are required to process high-grade ores. But now we are reduced to extracting our copper from ores that assay less than 1 percent, and soon we will have nothing better than 0.1 percent. It takes a very sophisticated technology to deal with low-grade ores, a technology that only

a large population of technologically advanced people can muster. So it is for many other materials—special steels, solid-state
electronic devices, and highly purified chemicals. Our many
technologies form an incredible network of mutual support,
mutual dependence. If this network were disrupted by thermo-
nuclear war, which, at the same time, reduced the population
to a small fraction of its former size, and then that fraction had
to scratch out a living under conditions of severe poverty, it is
doubtful if our kind of technology would ever be rebuilt. To
do so would require great capital expenditures over several
decades. Capital is income deferred. A poor people is under-
standably reluctant to defer much income. If several decades
are required before there is a substantial payoff, the problem of
rebuilding technology following the crash becomes a problem
of making sacrifices for posterity. That is always a hard thing
to do; the poor find it almost impossibly hard.

Moreover, what would be the emotional "set" of humanity
following "the bomb" or the crash? Is it not conceivable that
the survivors might just decide that what we call "civilization"
is not worth rebuilding? And who would then say that they
were wrong?[13]

No civilization has ever recovered after ruining its environment. The civilizations of Egypt, of the Tigris-Euphrates valley,
of the Indus River, and of Rome were replaced by other civilizations from the outside. If we ruin the whole world, where is the
"outside" to renew our civilization? On all counts, it looks as
though our civilization, once fallen, will never be replaced by
another of comparable quality. If we esteem what we have we
must somehow defuse both the nuclear bomb and the population bomb.[14]

Population can be controlled only by making hard decisions.
There is no fundamental reason why we cannot do it. The ques-

tion is, who is the *we* that acts? Policy must revolve around this identification.

The basic fact of our world is that there are many *wes*. The number shows no signs of diminishing. There are now about three times as many countries in the United Nations as there were when the organization was formed some thirty years ago. Some of them are merely old nations newly admitted, but many are nations newly created by the fission of old ones. No instance of fusion has occurred during this thirty years, but fission continues.

Each nation insists on its sovereignty. What does that mean? The sovereignty claimed boils down to this: a nation's spokesmen let us know what they are responsible *for*—but say nothing of what they are responsible *to*. They say they are responsible for the survival and continued multiplication of their people, but they do not acknowledge responsibility to anyone for what that growth does to the rest of the world and to the future. That is true of poor nations and rich nations alike. Talk about "Spaceship Earth" is peppered with loud claims of "rights" coupled with equally vehement disclaimers of Frankelian responsibility.

The fact of national sovereignty, as it exists at present, had better be accepted. But when a nation denies that it has any responsibility to make its population match the carrying capacity of its own land, it would be foolish for other nations to accept responsibility for keeping alive millions of people the procreation of whom they had nothing to do with. Yet that is what spokesmen for the "Third World" (the current euphemism for "poor countries") asserted at the United Nations conference on population in Bucharest in 1974. In effect, what Third World spokesmen said was this: "We in the poor countries have the right to produce as many children as we want to: you in the rich have the responsibility of keeping them alive." Out of that conference, and one on food in Rome later in the same year, came the proposal for setting up a World Food Bank. The operational rules of the proposed "bank" are a blueprint for disaster.

In the first place the word *bank* is a misnomer. Two generations ago there were a score of countries that were significant grain exporters by virtue of the fact that they produced an excess. Now there are only five: Argentina, Australia, Canada, France, and the United States. Although food production is increasing nearly everywhere, there is almost no increase in per capita food production except in those five countries, so we must assume that the future will be as bleak as the recent past. That means that the depositors of the bank would always be one group of countries, and the withdrawers another. This arrangement hardly corresponds to the workings of a bank: it is more like a siphon.

The proposal, then, amounts to this: that we build world policy on the ideal Karl Marx stated in 1875, "From each according to his ability, to each according to his needs."[15] But this famous phrase merely defines the system of the commons: people take from a common store whatever they think they need.[16] The end result, if such a policy is continued indefinitely, will be a tragedy.[17] Figure 2 diagrams the scenario: we have only to change "external food book" to "world food bank." The nature of the ultimate population crash is a suitable subject for nightmares.

Predation and disease are the commonest controllers of population in other species. Human beings have no predators now, and disease has almost been conquered. Death is the commonest controlling event for other species; for death, we human beings can substitute non-birth. The technology of contraception, while less perfect than we would like, is quite adequate to the task. Our problem is to use this technology intensively and extensively enough to do the job.

If the tragedy of the commons is to be prevented each unit that claims sovereignty—each nation—must accept Frankelian responsibility and adjust its population to match the carrying capacity of its land. That does not mean that any nation need be self-sufficient with respect to all its material needs. No industrialized nation has within its own borders everything it needs—copper, chrome, bauxite, oil, vanadium, etc. But a properly run country will produce surpluses of some things, which it can then trade for what it lacks. Every country can be self-reliant (even though few or none can be totally self-sufficient). When a country has become self-reliant it can be said to be living within the carrying capacity of its land. Thus we see that the concept of carrying capacity in the human realm is significantly different than in the animal.

Since population and the standard of living are inversely related to each other, when population increases the material standard of living must fall, if a country is to continue to be self-reliant. Conversely, if a people want to "live higher on the hog" and still be self-reliant, they must find a way to reduce their population. There is no simple connection between the natural wealth of a nation and its per capita income. Some of the poorest nations of the world live in lands of great natural wealth—India, for instance. There are just too many people there; if India had only 75 million people (instead of her 600 million) her population density would be the same as that of the United States and life could be very comfortable.

The sight of starving millions in poor countries may move compassionate people to send food for the emergency. But *emergency* is usually a misnomer: it is not a temporary crisis but a permanent crunch (which fluctuates in intensity, of course). The intended effect of sending food is to save lives;

the more successfully this goal is met the greater the danger of an unintended side effect—the weakening of the springs of action that might otherwise lead a harassed people to bring population and carrying capacity into balance.

For a well-fed citizen of a wealthy nation to point out that a poor country will be better off in the long run without inputs of food from the outside inevitably leads to the charge that the advice is "self-serving." So it may be. But we must go behind that charge and ask: Does withholding food serve the needs of the needy as well *in the long run?*

When I was in India in 1970 I was gratified to learn that many educated Indians understand their situation very well. I was fortunate enough to have an hour's conference with a member of the Indian planning commission. He recounted his reaction to the events of 1965–66, when, for two years running, the United States sent ten million tons of grain to make up for a shortfall in Indian agriculture. It has been estimated that this saved the lives of 50 million Indians. With the second year's shipment President Johnson privately told the Indian leaders that they could expect no more. We could help in crises but not in crunches: the Indians had better learn to take care of themselves. My informant told me that he and others in government had been indignant at the time; but faced with necessity they exerted themselves to improve Indian agriculture, and did. The hard line taken by the United States may have been self-serving but it also served the needs of India, the greatest of which is the need to be self-reliant.

We will do little good in the international sphere until we recognize that the greatest need of a poor country is not material: call it psychological, moral, spiritual, or what you will. The basic issue is starkly raised in a story of personal heroism that unfolded in South America a few years ago. A plane carrying a Uruguayan rugby team crashed in the remote Andes, leaving most of the passengers alive. After they got a radio receiver working they listened day after day to news of the Chilean air force flying in search of them. Finally came the day when the small group of listeners outside the shattered plane heard that the search had been called off because the Chileans figured they could not possibly be alive. Most of the Uruguayans were inside the hull of the plane and had not heard the news. "What shall we tell the others?" one of the listeners asked.

"We musn't tell them," said Marcelo. "At least let them go on hoping."

"No," said Nicolich. "We must tell them. They must know the worst."

"I can't, I can't," said Marcelo, still sobbing into his hands.

"I'll tell them," said Nicolich, and he turned back toward the entrance to the plane.

He climbed through the hole in the wall of suitcases and rugby shirts, crouched at the mouth of the dim tunnel, and looked at the mournful faces which were turned toward him.

"Hey, boys," he shouted. "There's some good news! We just heard it on the radio. They've called off the search."

Inside the crowded cabin there was silence. As the hopelessness of their predicament enveloped them, they wept.

"Why the hell is that good news?" Páez shouted angrily at Nicolich.

"Because it means," he said, "that we're going to get out of here on our own."[18]

And they did get out. Not all of them. Many died. But if they had not heard the bad news, if they had stayed there waiting, waiting—*all* would have died.

This true story, I submit, bears a close resemblance to the moral situation of poor countries. The greatest gift we can give them is the knowledge that they are on their own.

For corroborative evidence, consider the contrasting cases of China and India. Fifty years ago these countries were equally overpopulated, equally miserable, and their futures looked equally bleak. During this period, particularly during the past twenty-five years, we have given massive aid to India. (So have other rich nations.) Because of a political falling-out we have given nothing to Maoist China (neither have any other nations, except the USSR, briefly). Today China is immensely better off, both physically and psychologically. She has not solved her population problem, but she is much closer than India to doing so. Millions of people died during China's time of troubles; but she had the great advantage of receiving no help from us. She was on her own, and she knew it. India, by contrast, was handicapped by our "help."

Help—what a dangerous word that is! It is not the name for an act; it is the name for an interpretation of an act. When the people in power in the United States sent soldiers and arms into Vietnam in the early 1960s, they genuinely thought they were helping the Vietnamese. When we of the industrial world built a dam on the Zambezi River in Africa and created Lake Kariba we called it "help," though it displaced 57,000 people from their ancestral farms and increased the extent of infection by schistosome worms.[19] When we sent pesticides—a loaded word, like "help"—to the cotton farmers of the Cañete Valley in Peru we called it "help," though the resultant destruction of the predators of the insect pests created a boomerang effect that nearly wiped out cotton growing in the valley.[20] And whenever amiable people fly hay into overpopulated deer country they too say they are "helping."

The word we are looking for is *intervention*; this is a neutral, descriptive word that leaves open the question of interpretating it. Feeding deer on winter-feeding grounds is intervention in the lives of the deer; it may help them, it may harm them. Killing predators is intervention. Building a dam is intervention; so also is sending people supplies of DDT, medicines, food, bombers, napalm, military advisers, agricultural experts, miracle grains, and Hollywood movies. There is no law of nature that says that every well-intentioned act of intervention deserves the name of "help." In fact, experience indicates that the contrary is closer to the truth. The effects of intervention must never be assumed: they remain to be proved.

We are lucky (and so are the recipients of our attentions) when our interventions are no worse than harmless. When our government buys the grain of American farmers and ships it to a starving and overpopulated country it certainly helps our farmers, our railroads, our grain elevator operators, and our shipowners to grow rich. It even helps a few bureaucrats to keep their jobs. But does it help the people of the nation in which we intervene? Does it help them not only today, but tomorrow and the day after? That remains to be proved.

Of course, leaving a country to its own devices does not insure that it will solve its problems. When political changes are called for—and to some extent they invariably are—it is hard to know what measures or events will facilitate the needed changes. But we should know by now that people on the outside are unlikely to be able to bring about a needed political change. About the only thing outside meddling can do is interfere with internal progress.

In every country, rich or poor, there is a great variety of opinion and talent. It is a mistake to say, as many do, that "poor countries demand this" or "poor countries demand that." A country is not an organism: it has no voice. People have voices: different people, different voices. The shrill and demanding voices heard in Budapest and Rome were only some of the voices of the Third World: they were the voices of self-selected spokesmen. If we meet their demands and set up a commons in food from which their countries can draw at will we will weaken the urge toward self-reliance; we will reward misguided prophets. But if we ignore these prophets they will lose in political power and other voices will be heard in their countries. Some of them may have answers that will do some good. A course of apparent non-action on our part may be the best way to encourage constructive action inside needy countries.

Population control—home-grown population control—is the greatest need. We may be able to help by offering rewards to countries that make progress in population control. If we adopt this policy we must be very clear in our own minds about this important matter: we must concern ourselves only with the end to be achieved and not with the means of achieving it. Means must match culture. Different cultures, different means. Among the means available for controlling family size and population are the following: sterilization, abortion, infanticide, civil penalties for over-large families, and delayed marriage associated with continence outside of marriage. Though it may not be obvious, polygamy also can reduce population growth. If one man has many wives (polygyny) it follows that many men have no wives. The wifeless men may patronize prostitutes, who are notoriously (and fortunately) relatively infertile, while wives gathered together in harems will not—despite all dreams of *machismo*—be as well serviced (to use the language of animal husbandry) as they would be in a monogamous society.

Few among us would approve all these ways of reducing the rate of population growth, yet every practice listed is followed some place in the world today. We could hardly be expected to recommend to others a practice we are unwilling to follow ourselves; but must we go out of our way to disapprove of an effective means of population control used with approval by another culture? Unfortunately many among us do just that. There seems to be a growing sentiment toward promoting the idea of universal human rights. In practice, any nation that adopts this position defines its own version of human rights as

the universal one. Universal human rights is an absolutist concept; basing international policy on this concept leads to ethical
imperialism.

We will fail in our intention if, in encouraging another nation to assume responsibility for the control of its own population, we are so arrogant as to dictate the means. Different means
fit different cultures. Furthermore we may even be mistaken in
the means we adopt in our own society, a truth we will discover
sooner if we encourage varied practices throughout the world
and then observe the varied successes to see what we can learn
of benefit to ourselves. Tolerance of differences is a virtue that
recommends itself to altruists, but it has merit for egoists as
well: those who admit that they may not have all the best answers can improve their ethics through vicarious experience.

4

Who Cares for Posterity?

Two CENTURIES AGO the American poet John Trumbull (1750–1831) posed a question that has ever since disturbed those who want to put a wholly rational foundation under conservation policy. Why, Trumbull asked, should people act

> ... as though there were a tie
> And obligation to posterity.
> We get them, bear them, breed, and nurse:
> What has posterity done for us?[1]

The question is surely an ethical one. One would think that philosophers who have been dealing with ethics for more than two thousand years would by this time have developed a rather impressive intellectual apparatus for dealing with the needs of posterity; but they have not. In a thought-provoking essay on "Technology and Responsibility," Hans Jonas points out that ethical literature is almost wholly individualistic: it is addressed to private conduct rather than to public policy.[2] Martin Buber epitomized this spirit well when he oriented his ethics around the *I–Thou* dyad.[3] That sounds fine until a close reading reveals

that the author means no more than *I–Thou, Here and Now.*
The standard ethical dialogue is between people who stand
face to face with each other, seeking a reasonable basis for reciprocal altruism. Posterity has no chance to show its face in
the here and now.

Except for Jonas's valuable comments, contemporary philosophy still evades the hard problem of caring for posterity's
interests. Probably no recent work is as well known or spoken
of with such awe as John Rawls's *A Theory of Justice,* so we
should see what this book has to say about "the problem of
justice between generations," as Rawls puts the problem.[4] In
§44 the author candidly admits that in his hopefully compre-
hensive system of analysis the problem "seems to admit of no
definite answer." One might suppose that he would then drop
the matter but he somehow manages to talk about it for another
fourteen pages without adding anything more positive than
statements such as "men have a natural duty to uphold and to
further just institutions." This pronouncement is less than revolutionary; it is hardly operational. Perhaps we have expected too
much from philosophers.[5] Can economists throw any more
light on the problem of posterity?

Time is of the essence. In cost–benefit analysis we attempt to
list and evaluate all the costs (negative benefits); similarly with
all the (positive) benefits; then we strike a balance for the
whole, on which action can be based. If the balance is plus we
go ahead; if minus, we stop. The decision is simple if costs and
benefits are encountered at practically the same moment. But
what if they are separated by a considerable gap in time? What
if the benefits come now and the costs do not turn up for a
generation? Contrariwise, what if costs have to be paid now
for benefits that come later? How do we balance costs against
benefits when time is interposed between the two?

To begin with let us take up the benefits-first problem, which throws an interesting light on human nature. When the High Aswan Dam was proposed for the Nile only its expected benefits were publicized: the additional electricity it would generate and the additional land that could be irrigated with the impounded water. The huge financial cost of the dam was acknowledged, but the world was told that it would be well worth it. It would bring the blessings of "development" to the poor people of Egypt.

People were not told certain other costs that were well known to some agricultural experts. Agriculture in the Nile below Aswan had always depended on a yearly flooding of the flat fields. This flooding accomplished two things: it leached out the salts accumulated from the preceding year's evaporation of irrigation water, and it left behind one millimeter of silt, which served as fertilizer for the next year's crops. This system of agriculture had been successful for six thousand years—a unique record of long-term success. Now technologists proposed to put an end to it.

Had there been any national or international debate on the subject the debaters should have wrestled with this question: Do today's short-term benefits of more electricity and more agricultural land in the upper reaches of the river outweigh tomorrow's losses in the lower valley resulting from salination and loss of fertility? The gains are necessarily short term: all dam-lakes eventually silt up and become useless as generators of electricity and sources of abundant water. The process usually takes only a century or two, and often much less. No economically feasible method has ever been found for reclaiming a silted-up dam-lake. The loss from salination of irrigated land is also virtually permanent; treatment requires periodic flooding, but that is what the High Aswan Dam was designed to prevent. The Tigris–Euphrates valley, in which irrigation was practiced for centuries, was ruined by salination two thousand years ago—and it is still ruined.

How a cost–benefit balance would have been struck had these facts been known to the decision makers we do not know. Probably their reaction would have been that of Mr. Micawber in *David Copperfield*: "Something will turn up." Such is the faith of the technological optimists. "Eat, drink, and be merry —for tomorrow we will find a solution to today's problems. We will learn how to dredge out dam-ponds—economically. We will learn how to desalinate farmland—economically. Don't wait until we've solved these problems. Plunge ahead! Science will find an answer in time."

Curiously, economists have more confidence in science and technology than scientists do. Could it be that too much knowledge is a bad thing? Should conservatism in ecological matters be labeled a vice rather than a virtue? So say the technological optimists.

Well, the High Aswan Dam has been built now, and the returns are coming in. They are worse than expected. There has not been time for appreciable salination or significant loss of soil fertility—which no one expected this soon anyway—but other disadvantages we had not foreseen have turned up. Water behind the dam is rising more slowly than had been hoped, because of unexpected leakage into surrounding rock strata and greater than expected evaporation from the surface of the lake. The present steady flow of water in irrigation channels (instead of the former intermittent flow) favors snails that carry parasitic worms. As a result, the painful and debilitating disease of schistosomiasis is more widespread among Egyptians now. There are medical measures that can be taken against the disease and sanitary measures to combat the snails, but both cost money, which is what the Egyptians are short of. In addition, the reduction of the flow of the Nile has opened the delta to erosion by the currents of the Mediterranean; as a result, precious delta farmland is now being swept into the sea. And the stoppage of the annual fertilization of the eastern Mediterranean by flood-borne silt has destroyed 95 percent of the local sardine fisheries.[6] The dam is proving a disaster, and sooner than anyone had thought.

Mr. Micawber, where are you now?

We come now to the opposite problem, that of weighing present costs against future benefits. For this question there is a rational economic theory. Let us see if it is adequate.

Suppose I offer to sell you something that will be worth $100 ten years from now: how much should you be willing to pay for it? If you are the standard "economic man," equipped with a hand calculator, you will say something like this: "Well, let me see: assuming the interest rate for money stays at 6 percent, I cannot afford to pay you more than $55.84 for this opportunity. So if you want to close the deal you'll have to accept $55.84 or a bit less to get me to opt for $100 ten years from now."

The reasoning is as follows. A person with some money to spare can either put it in the bank at 6 percent interest or invest it in this enterprise. Put in the bank, $55.84 (at compound interest) will amount to $100 ten years later: the proposed investment should be able to do that well. If the investor thinks the proposal is speculative he will make a lower bid (i.e., expect a higher rate of interest). If he is worried about inflation (and thinks he knows another investment that is inflation-proof) he will demand a still lower price.

In economic terms, we "discount" the future value at a discount rate (rate of interest), calling the discounted value the "present value." The present value of $100 ten years from now at a discount rate of 6 percent is $55.84; if the discount rate is

10 percent the present value is only $38.55. The formula for these calculations is:

$$\text{Present value} = \text{Future value} \div e^{bt}$$

where: e = base of natural logarithms (ln)
   $b = ln\,(1 + \text{interest rate})$
and t = time

The economic theory of discounting is a completely rational theory. For short periods of time it gives answers that seem intuitively right. For longer periods, we are not so sure.

A number of years ago I decided to plant a redwood tree in my backyard.[7] As I did so I mused, "What would my economist friends say to this? Would they approve? Or would they say I was an economic fool?"

The seedling cost me $1.00. When mature the tree would (at the then current prices) have $14,000 worth of lumber in it—but it would take two thousand years to reach that value. Calculation showed that the investment of so large a sum of money as $1.00 to secure so distant a gain would be justified only if the going rate of interest was no more than 0.479 percent per year. So low a rate of interest has never been known. Plainly I was being a rather stupid "economic man" in planting that tree. *But I planted it.*

The theory of discounting scratches only the surface of the problem. What about the quid pro quo? The quid ($1.00) is mine to pay; but who gets the quo, two thousand years from now? Not I, certainly. And it is most unlikely that any of my direct descendants will get it either, history being what it is. The most I can hope for is that an anonymous posterity will benefit by my act. Almost the only benefit I get is the thought that posterity will benefit—a curious sort of quo indeed. Why bother?

I am beginning to suspect that rationality—as we now con-

76]   THE LIMITS OF ALTRUISM

ceive it—may be insufficient to secure the end we desire, namely
taking care of the interests of posterity.[8] (At least, some of us
desire that.) I can illustrate my point with a true story, which
I shall embellish with a plausible historical explanation.

During the Second World War certain fragments of information, and fragments of wood, coming out of China led the
California botanist Ralph Chaney to believe that the dawn
redwood, which had been thought to be extinct for hundreds
of thousands of years, was still in existence. Fortunately Chaney
was a person of initiative and independent means, and he
promptly set out for China to look for the tree. Getting to the
interior of this war-torn country was no small accomplishment,
but he did it. He found the tree. It was in an area that had
suffered severe deforestation for several thousand years, and
there were fewer than a thousand dawn redwoods left. They
were still being cut down for fuel and cabinetmaking. Most of
the living specimens were in temple courtyards—and thereby
hangs our tale.

What is so special about being in a temple courtyard? Just
this: it makes the object sacred. The word *sacred* is not easy to
define, but whatever we mean by it we mean something that
stands outside the bounds of rationality, as ordinarily understood. Let me illustrate this by a fictional conversation between
a priest and a peasant in a Chinese temple a thousand years
ago. Knowing almost nothing of Chinese social history I cannot make the conversation idiomatically correct, but I think
the sense of it will be right.

A peasant from the deforested countryside, desperate for
fuel to cook his rice, has slipped into a temple courtyard and
is breaking twigs off the dawn redwood when he is appre-
hended by the priest.
"Here, here! You can't do that!"
"But, honorable sir, I have to. See, I have a little rice in this
bowl, but it is uncooked. I can't eat it that way. I'm starving.

If you'll only let me have a few twigs I can cook my rice and
live another day."

"I'm sorry," says the priest, "but it is forbidden. This tree
is sacred. No one is allowed to harm it."

"But if I don't get this fuel I will die."

"That's too bad: the tree is sacred. If everybody did what
you are trying to do there soon wouldn't be any tree left."

The peasant thinks a few moments and then gets very
angry: "Do you mean to tell me that the life of a mere tree
is more valuable than the life of a human being?"

Now this is a very Westernized, twentieth-century question; I doubt that an ancient Chinese would have asked it.
But if he had, how would the priest have replied? He might
have repeated his assertion that the tree was sacred; or he might
have tried to frighten the peasant by saying that touching it
would bring bad luck to him in the future. That which is sacred
or taboo is generally protected by legends that tend to make the
taboo operational: bad luck, the evil eye, the displeasure of the
gods. Are such stories consciously concocted because the idea
of posterity is too remote to be effective? Or is it just a coinci-
dence that objects so protected do survive for posterity's enjoy-
ment? Whatever the case, being treated as sacred can protect an
object against destruction by impoverished people who might
otherwise discount the future in a simplistically rational way.

Once the peasant realized that the tree was sacred (or that its
destruction would bring him bad luck) he would probably have
slunk out of the courtyard. But suppose we continue to endow
him with twentieth-century sentiments and see what happens.

"Sir," says the peasant, "your position is a self-serving one
if I ever heard such. It's all well and good for you to be so
thoughtful of posterity, for you get your three square meals a
day no matter what. But what about me? Why do I have to
serve posterity while you stuff your belly? Where's your sense
of justice?"

"You're right," admits the priest. "I *am* the beneficiary of special privilege. There's only one thing to do," he says, as he takes off his clothes, "and that is to trade positions. Take your clothes off and trade with me! From now on you are the priest and I am a peasant."

That is a noble gesture—but surely the point is obvious? The gesture solves nothing. The next day, when the priest-turned-peasant comes begging for wood, the peasant-turned-priest must refuse him. If he doesn't the tree will soon be destroyed.

But the dawn redwood did survive. The conversation was fictional but the event—saving the trees by labeling some of them sacred—is true. The ginkgo tree was also saved in this way: it was known only in temple courtyards when Western men first found it in China. Special privilege preserved the trees in the face of vital demands made by an impoverished people.

Are we in the West capable of such severity? I know of only two stories of this sort, both from the USSR. The first dates from 1921, a time of famine there.[9] An American journalist visited a a refugee camp on the Volga where almost half the people had already died of starvation. Noticing sacks of grain stacked in great mounds in an adjacent field, he asked the patriarch of the refugee community why the people did not simply overpower the lone soldier guarding the grain and help themselves. The patriarch explained that the sacks contained seed for planting the next season. "We do not steal from the future," he said.

Much the same thing happened again in the Second World War.[10] The siege of Leningrad by the Germans lasted 900 days, killing about a quarter of the population of three million. The cold and starving inhabitants had to eat dogs, cats, rats, and dried glue from furniture joints and wallpaper. All this time truckloads of edible seeds in containers were in storage in the All-Union Institute of Plant Industry. The seeds were a precious repository of genetic variety for Russian agriculture in the future. These seeds were never touched, though hundreds of thousands of people died.

Do these stories show that starving people are just naturally noble and take the long view? No. As was pointed out in chapter 1, the behavior of people in prison camps shows that the opposite is the case. Altruism evaporates as egoism takes over.[11] It is egoism of the crudest sort: people will sacrifice every promise of tomorrow for the merest scrap of food today. It is as though the interest rate for discounting the future approached infinity.

Under severe survival conditions morality disappears, as became evident in an experiment carried out by American physiologists during the Second World War.[12] Foreseeing the need to treat starving victims of European concentration camps after the Germans were driven back, and recognizing that there was too little sound physiological knowledge, American scientists called for volunteers to take part in starvation experiments. Some conscientious objectors, members of the Church of the Brethren, volunteered. They were extremely idealistic young men, but as their ribs started to show, their ideals evaporated. They stole food from any place they could get it, including from one another. Many people do not like to face this sort of reality about human nature, but thoughtful religious men have known it for centuries. Thomas Aquinas summarized the situation very well when he said, "Necessity knows no law."[13]

It is futile to ask starving people to act against their own self-interest as they see it, which is an exclusively short-term self-interest. In a desperate community long-term interests can be protected only by institutional means: soldiers and policemen. These agents will be reliable only if they are fed up to some minimum level, higher than the average of the starving population. In discounting the future a man's personal discount rate is directly related to the emptiness of his stomach. Those who are the guardians of future stores must be put in a favored position to keep their personal discount rates low—that is, to make it possible for them to believe in, and protect, the future.

In a prosperous society the interests of posterity may often be served by the actions of a multitude of people. These actions are (or at least seem to be) altruistic. That cannot happen in a desperately needy society. When necessity is in the saddle we dare not expect altruism from "the people." Only institutions can then take actions that would be called altruistic were individuals to perform them. "An institution," as George Berg has pointed out, "can be considered as an anticipating device designed to pay off its members now for behavior which will benefit and stabilize society later."[14] An army, a police force, and a priesthood are institutions that *can* serve the needs of posterity —which they may or may not do.

Moralists try to achieve desired ends by exhorting people to be moral. They seldom succeed; and the poorer the society (other things being equal) the less their success. Institutionalists try to achieve desired ends by the proper design of institutions, allowing for the inescapable moral imperfection of the people on whose services institutions must depend. The Cardinal Rule is not violated: institution-designers count on people acting egoistically.

If there is complete equality of position and power in a needy society the interests of posterity are unlikely to be taken care of. Seeds for the future will be used for food today by a hungry people acting egoistically. To serve the future a few individuals must be put in the special position of being egoistically rewarded for protecting the seeds against the mass of people not enjoying special privilege. Well-fed soldiers acting egoistically (to preserve their institutional right to be well fed) can protect posterity's interests against the egoistic demands of today's hungry people. It is not superior morality that is most likely to serve posterity but an institutional design that makes wise use of special privilege.

I am not pleading for more special privilege in our own country. So far as posterity's interests are concerned the richer the country the less need it has for special privilege. We are rich. But I do plead for tolerance and understanding of special privilege in other countries, in poor countries. Political arrangements can never be wholly independent of the circumstances of life. We have long given lip service to this principle, recognizing that illiteracy, poverty, and certain traditions make democracy difficult. If we wish to protect posterity's interests in poor countries we must understand that distributional justice is a luxury that cannot be afforded by a country in which population overwhelms the resource base.

In a poor country, if all people are equally poor—if there is no special privilege—the future will be universally discounted at so high a rate that it will practically vanish. Posterity will be cheated; and being cheated it will, in its turn, be still poorer and will discount the future at an even higher rate. Thus a vicious cycle is established. Only special privilege can break this cycle in a poor country. We need not positively approve of special privilege; but we can only do harm if, like the missionaries of old, we seek to prevent it.

Special privilege does not insure that the interests of posterity will be taken care of in a poor country; it merely makes it possible. Those enjoying special privilege may find it in their hearts to safeguard the interests of posterity against the necessarily—and forgivably—short-sighted egoism of the desperately poor who are under the natural necessity of discounting the future at a ruinous rate. We will serve posterity's interests better if we give up the goal of diminishing special privilege in poor countries. We should seek instead to persuade the privileged to create altruistic institutions that can make things better for posterity, thus diminishing the need for special privilege in the future.

Special privilege may be *pro tempore*, as it is for drafted or enlisted soldiers (in the stories told of the USSR); or it may extend over generations by virtue of hereditary privilege. The privileged always seek to make privilege hereditary. There is much to be said against hereditary privilege, from both biological and political points of view; but it has a peculiar psychological merit from the point of view of posterity, a merit pointed out by Edmund Burke (1729–1797) when he said: "People will not look forward to posterity who never look backward to their ancestors."[15] The image evoked by this old-fashioned voice of conservatism is one of landed gentry or nobility, reared in baronial halls lined with the pictures of ancestors, looking out over comfortable estates, which they are determined to keep intact against the demands of the less fortunate, so that their children may enjoy what they enjoy. In some psychological sense posterity and ancestors fuse together in the service of an abstraction called "family."

If Burke's psychology is right (and I think it is), he points to several ways in which posterity may be served despite the strictures of hardheaded economics. A society in which prosperity is less than universal may institutionalize special privilege. (The desired result is not guaranteed: when ill used, special privilege can have the opposite effect, of course.) Where wealth is sufficiently great and more equitably distributed, a society that held Burke's assertion to be true would be expected to modify its institutions in a number of ways. Obviously it would see to it that the teaching of history played a large role in education.

Less obviously, a society interested in posterity might decide that the policy of encouraging a high degree of mobility in the labor force should be reversed. There is considerable anecdotal evidence to show that a person's identification with the past is significantly strengthened by exposure during childhood to the sight of enduring artifacts: family portraits, a stable dwelling place, even unique trees.[16] It is harder for a mobile family to achieve this unconscious identification with the past. It is the conventional wisdom of economics that labor mobility improves the productivity of a nation. In the short run that may be true; but if the Burkean argument presented here is sound it means that short-term economic efficiency is purchased at the expense of long-term failure to conserve resources.

One further and rather curious point needs to be made about this argument. If I believe it to be true that locational stability encourages the identification of the past with the future, that belief may have little direct effect on my own actions because my childhood is now beyond reach. Such a "belief" would be a conscious one, and it seems that only unconscious beliefs have much power to cause actions that run contrary to the dictates of simple rationality. I cannot willfully create within myself the psychological identification whose praises I sing. The most I can do (if I am powerful and clever enough) is modify the environment of other people—of children now growing up—so that they will unconsciously come to give preference to the interests of posterity.

Here is a curious question: if, because of my own childhood I myself lack a strong feeling for place and ancestry (and hence for posterity), what would lead me to try to inculcate it in others by working to modify their childhood experiences? Isn't this process a sort of lifting one's self by one's bootstraps, a sort of second-order altruism? The problem of posterity is rich in puzzles!

Whatever the answer may be to questions like these, this much should be clear: once a society loses a keen concern for posterity, regaining such a sense will be the work not of a few years but of a generation or more. If civilization should collapse worldwide, the second tragedy would be the loss of the will to rebuild it. Under the inescapable condition of dire poverty, augmented no doubt by a rejection of the past that had caused the collapse, effective concern for posterity would virtually dis-appear—not forever, perhaps, but until historical developments we cannot possibly foresee rekindled a concern for social con-tinuity.

In the light of this conclusion questions of another sort should be raised. Do we yet have the knowledge needed to in-sure the indefinite survival of any political unit? Do we yet know how to prevent the collapse that overtook all previous civilizations? If we do, then it is safe to create One World (if we can); but if we do not, it is not advisable even to try. If col-lapse is still an inescapable part of the life cycle of political units then posterity would be poorly served by a fusing of all present states into one. We should instead preserve enough of the economic and social barriers between groupings of human-ity so that the cancer of collapse can be localized.[17]

If knowledge of local wretchedness in distant states should lead us altruistically to create a resource commons we would thereby become a party to the ultimate metastasis of collapse. If our understanding of the physiology and pathology of po-litical organizations is less than total, an overriding concern for the needs of the present generation can lead to a total sacrifice of the interests of posterity. I submit that our knowledge of the laws of political behavior is less than total. I will return to this matter in the last chapter.

5

Who Dealt This Hand?

THE CENTRAL REALITY that must be accepted by those who elect to play a card game is inequity: the hands that are dealt out are not equal in value. Inequity also prevails in the distribution of environmental riches among nations. Soil fertility, climate, scenery, fresh water, the potential for hydroelectric power, coal, petroleum, and other minerals are distributed very unevenly over the earth and among nations. To the inequities created by the natural forces of geology and climatology are added the accidents of history that help to determine the way national boundaries are drawn and the present stage of industrial development of the various nations.

The ability to produce food is one of the important differences among nations. Some 90 percent of the world's food for human beings is produced and consumed locally and does not enter into international trade. Exports are "marginal" to production; but as is so often true, marginal factors are important. Exports play a decisive role in determining prices, the prosperity of farmers, and the distribution of international power, real or potential. So let us look at the most important facts about the export of food grains at the present time (Table 6).

TABLE 6

Food Dependency

| Area | Population in 1976 | | Net exports of cereal grains, in million metric tons | |
	Total, in millions	Doubling time, in yrs.	1948–52	1974
Africa	432	25	− .37	− 7
Asia, except Japan	2,364	27	− 3	−28
Japan	112	64	− 3	−19
Europe, except France	422	122	−20	−45
France	53	88	− 1	+17
Latin America, except Argentina	307	26	− 2	−12
Argentina	26	50	+ 4	+11
Australia	14	50	+ 3	+ 7
Canada	23	54	+ 8	+12
United States	222	54	+14	+65

Notes

Immediate source of data: 1976 World Population Estimates, published by The Environmental Fund, 1302 Eighteenth St., N.W., Washington, D.C. 20036.

Ultimate sources: populations from the International Statistical Program Center, U.S. Bureau of the Census; grain exports from the UNFAO Trade Yearbooks, vols. 14 and 28.

In the last two columns a *minus* sign indicates a net *import*.

In 1974 there were only 18 countries with positive net exports of cereal grains: Kenya, Malawi, South Africa, Bhutan, Nepal, Burma, Thailand, Canada, the United States, Argentina, Uruguay, Denmark, Sweden, Romania, Hungary, Australia, France, and the USSR.

Roughly speaking, one ton of grain will support five people for one year on a wholly vegetarian diet.

Note that four great regions of the world are net importers: Africa, Asia, Europe, and most of Latin America. Two countries not listed separately in the table deserve comment. First, the USSR, which is on a knife-edge, with imports outrunning exports one year, the reverse another. The balance for the Soviet Union is determined principally by three factors: the weather, the quality of the agricultural decisions made by the central bureaucracy, and the amount of grain fed to animals (another central decision).

China deserves special comment, too, because of a widespread misconception about her situation. Enthusiasts often assert that the Maoist regime converted China from a net importer of grain to a net exporter. That is not true; she is a net importer now, and there is nothing in the cards to suggest that the situation will change significantly in the foreseeable future.

The source of this misconception is easy to pinpont. It arises from the change in the American public's attitude toward a foreign government and the tendency of public opinion to swing like a pendulum from one extreme to another. In a parallel instance, a bit earlier in history, in the 1920s the Soviet Union, newly born as a socialist country, was viewed as all bad by the generality of Americans. In the '30s a reaction among the young, the radicals, and the self-styled intellectuals led to the opposing view that the USSR could do no wrong. Before the decade was out a number of keen observers, notable among whom was George Orwell, exposed this illusion. Since then the amplitude of the swings of public opinion about this country has been damped.

The public view of China seems to be following the same course. In the minds of many Americans during the '50s and '60s she could do no good; then the young, the radical, and the self-styled intellectuals rebelled and thought that Mao's country could do no wrong. No doubt the truth lies somewhere between. As concerns food production and population control China has made commendable progress, but she is not out of the woods. Her rate of population growth, as near as we can make out, is still more than 2 percent per year—higher than that of any country in Europe except Albania (also a Marxist country). As for food, China does export some grain each year; but she imports more than she exports. In 1974, for instance, her net imports of cereal grains amounted to 2.8 million metric tons. At one ton of grain for every five people that would be enough to feed 14 million people on a wholly vegetarian diet. For a large country that fairly recently suffered devastating famines that is not bad: it means that only 1.5 percent of the population is, so to speak, dependent on food from the outside. Imports vary from year to year, and it is hard to read trends, but the seven years leading up to 1974 give no evidence of a downward trend. Imports may even be increasing.[1] If the unfavorable weather some climatologists are predicting for the Northern Hemisphere becomes a reality China will soon be in deep trouble. But so will many other countries.

Of all the nations in the world the one most dependent on food import is Japan, which imported 19 million net tons of cereal grains in 1974—enough to feed 85 percent of the Japanese (assuming a wholly vegetarian diet). This percentage does not tell the whole story for several reasons: some of the grain was fed to livestock, with the usual 80 to 90 percent loss of calories; non-cereal imports (e.g., soybeans) are also important to the Japanese; and these island people get a great deal of their food from the sea. Even without an exact figure on Japan's dependency, it is clear that the Japanese could not survive at their present population density and level of affluence without very large imports of grain.

Out of 157 countries only 18 (11 percent) export more cereal grain than they import. All the rest, save Namibia, are net importers. Twelve percent of the world's people live in grain-exporting countries, 88 percent in importing countries. In order of importance the five major exporters are: the United States, France, Canada, Argentina, and Australia. These countries, which have only 8 percent of the world's population, produce 92 percent of the grain that enters the export market. The United States alone accounts for 53 percent of the exports. The total net exports, 122 million metric tons, would be enough to keep 610 million vegetarians alive.

It is bad enough that so many—so many nations, so many people—are dependent on so few farmers in a few countries for their continued existence and well-being. What is even more alarming is the trend shown in the comparison of the last two columns of Table 6. In the past quarter of a century the difference between exporting and importing regions has become more pronounced. There is every reason to believe that the contrast will continue to become greater. Some 3.2 billion people live in poor areas with a high dependency on food imports (Asia, Africa, and Latin America). Their rate of reproduction is such that they will (if present trends continue) double their numbers in 27 years. By such time the people in the principal food-exporting nations—only about one-tenth as many, 338 million people—will have increased their aggregate population by less than a third (an increase of 133 million among the exporters compared to a 3,215 million increase among the importers). Any comfort we may find in food statistics is not to be found in these trends.

Who dealt this hand anyway? This is no way to run a world! Were we to play the "If I were God" game we would no doubt distribute food-producing ability according to local need, thus cutting down on transportation costs and wastes, and diminishing the political dangers of dependency. While we were playing the game we would no doubt redistribute the various minerals more equitably, too. And we certainly would see to it that no population grew beyond the carrying capacity of its land. Thus we would put an end to misery, as well as to the cries for help from distant places.

But we are not God, and we cannot redeal the hand: we must play the one that lies before us. Part of the dealing in the past was done by geology: you cannot grow Iowa's corn on the rocks of the Galapagos. The world's best soil is found in two sorts of regions: in the floodplains of rivers and at the terminuses of ancient glaciers. Glaciated regions are found only in the Northern Hemisphere. Geology determined the distribution of both kinds of soil and paid no attention to national needs.

Our hand was dealt in part by our ignorant and occasionally malevolent ancestors. In their ecological ignorance they cut down almost all the cedars of Lebanon. Mismanagement enlarged the deserts of northwestern India, Afghanistan, Iran, and northern Africa. The Mediterranean basin rather generally is a semi-disaster area created by man's ignorance. The eastern seaboard of the United States has lost much of its fertility for the same reason. The dust bowl centering in western Oklahoma and Kansas is also a human creation. The ruin of hillsides subjected to slash-and-burn agriculture in Central America had its origin in human error. And so on, almost *ad infinitum*. But we cannot remake the past; we cannot punish our ancestors. We have to play the hand as we get it. (If we are concerned about intergenerational justice we should seek to pass a better hand on to *our* posterity.)

In still another sense, we have been given a hand we have got to accept: in the historical–political sense. Americans are lucky in that they live in a fairly new country that was initially rich and has not yet been spoiled much by human beings. By contrast, contemporary Spaniards have to make do with a land that was ruined by shortsighted sheepherders some five hundred years ago, while those who live in the Sahel of Africa are stuck with a terrain that never did have much carrying capacity.

As was said earlier, in the human context it is wise to broaden the concept of carrying capacity to include the idea of self-reliance. Using a narrow definition of carrying capacity, both Spain and the Sahel have exceeded their proper carrying capacity; with a broader definition Spain looks pretty good. She is blessed with considerable tourist attractions: the Alhambra, the Costa Brava, Mallorca, the Prado, and so on. By paying for imports with experiences of beauty she can do pretty well. Saleable beauty is part of the carrying capacity, humanly defined.

The Sahel is another matter. It has virtually nothing to offer the rest of the world. Yet, as a result of past mismanagement (for which so many people are responsible that it is pointless to assign guilt) this broad band across Africa below the Sahara now has about 25 million people living in an area that, under proper management, has a true carrying capacity of perhaps five million.[2] How did this predicament come about? And what should we do about it?

International intervention, always risky, is doubly so when there is no responsible sovereign to deal with, as is the case in the Sahel. This region is occupied by no single nation, but contains portions of several nations, with nomads moving from one to another. But if it were a single nation, would it be wise for it to swell to five times its carrying capacity? Or for the outside world to encourage it to?

In a card game a man who bets too much on his hand is soon ruined. In the game of life can a nation that demands more than the carrying capacity of its land yields justifiably expect to escape the consequent ruin and suffering? If our compassion tempts us to slip the losers a few perishable jokers (e.g., food aid), are we really doing them, their environment, and their posterity a favor?

The Galapagos Islands have a resident human population of about four thousand, or one person for every two square kilometers. If these islands were as heavily populated as Java they would have over four million inhabitants. But what could so great a number live on? (And what would happen to the exotic animals and plants that constitute the principal wealth of these islands in the eyes of the world?)

In a rational management of the world, carrying capacity would be the prime datum for distributing people. For historical reasons the present distribution of peoples is not rational. Twenty-five million people in the Sahel is almost as irrational as four million in the Galapagos. What should be done about irrational distribution? We can dream of erasing all national boundaries, shuffling the people, and then redistributing them according to rational principles; but this proposal is clearly utopian in the pejorative sense. The peace of the world is on a hair trigger; we dare not consider anything so radical as the destruction of national sovereignties at this time.

We can ship food to people who live in overpopulated lands. The counterproductiveness of that policy has already been dealt with in chapter 2: it creates a ratchet effect that escalates the suffering to ever higher levels.

We might import the excess people into our own country. That would be the mirror image of the foreign aid error. If the United States took this project on as its duty, we would have to make way for about two thousand million poor people inside our borders—about forty people per existing family. The yearly increase of new poor in the world is about sixty million, so each year each American family would have to adopt another immigrant. Immigration as a solution for population problems is quixotic. Following this proposal to a fractional degree would not do the United States or any other country any good in the long run. The fraction admitted as immigrants from a poor country would soon be replaced by new births in that country; and the immigrant fraction would no doubt increase the birth-rate in the recipient country.

In the past, conquest of one country by another might have been a solution to overpopulation. I say *might* because I doubt if this solution was ever very practical for the neediest countries. Occasionally a poor but militaristic country might overwhelm a rich country, kill most of its inhabitants, and appropriate its wealth. The option of conquest is no longer open to the poor. Modern warfare is so expensive that even the richest nations cannot afford it: the 18-day Yom Kippur war in the Mideast in 1973 threatened to bankrupt the two nations who were financing it, the United States and the USSR.

Could a wise and compassionate God recommend any course of action to a nation except that of becoming self-reliant? If not, then the only remaining question is how fast can the country become self-reliant, and how much damage is done during the transition period? For damage will be done: it is of the essence of the concept of carrying capacity that the longer carrying capacity is exceeded the greater the damage, and the greater the proportion of this damage that is permanent. Posterity enters into the problem the moment we try to mitigate the suffering caused by overbidding a poor hand. And posterity is not far off. An example will make the point clear.

In 1974 the floods in Bangladesh were twice as bad as "normal" (the reason for the quotation marks will be made clear presently). Unnumbered thousands of lives were lost. In the popular press it was said that drowning, disease, and starvation were the "causes" of the deaths, but almost no deaths would have occurred had the population of Bangladesh been a tenth as great. Because there are too many Bengali for the small amount of land that is safe to live on, millions are forced to live on the floodplains of the Ganges and Brahmaputra rivers. Periodic flooding is certain, and loss of life is a necessary consequence of the overpopulation that forces people to live in such places.

But in the popular press, nobody ever dies of overpopulation: it is unthinkable.[3] So we say people die of starvation, drowning, disease, civil disorder, and countless other acceptable "causes." Taboo determines language, and language controls perception.

Overpopulation was involved in a second, subtler way in these deaths. Great floods are not really normal: they are to a large extent caused by man. God may send the rain, but how fast the water gets to the plains is determined by what man does to the highlands. In undisturbed mountains the soil trapped around tree roots acts as an absorbing sponge, delaying the flow of water to the rivers below.

Remove trees from steep slopes and a chain of destructive processes will ensue. Exposed soil is soon washed down the hillsides, increasing the volume of the rivers. Loss of absorptive capacity increases the speed of the flooding and the height of the crest. If there are irrigation systems below, they may be filled up with silt, and their walls may be broken. Dams will also be silted up, and their useful life will be shortened. Once soil is lost from steep hillsides it never comes back—not in human historical terms at any rate. (Over geological time it may.) So the mountain people with fewer trees and less soil are poorer than ever.

The mountains above Bangladesh are the Himalayas. Nepal, Bhutan, and Assam are among the countries nestled on those slopes. For some decades now these people have been increasing by more than two percent per year—that is, doubling in population every 35 years or less. The reasons are the usual ones: better medicine, better health, better nutrition, and to some extent

better agriculture. One can hardly begrudge people these blessings: but notice the consequences.

People do not live by bread alone; they need fuel also—fuel
to cook their food and (if they are lucky) a bit of fuel to heat
their homes. In most mountainous countries the only fuel available is wood. Energy deprivation is followed by deforestation,
and deforestation by soil erosion. The land below is damaged,
and the prospects of posterity in the highlands are diminished.
And all because too many people are living in the hill country.

In a very real sense the loss of life in the Bangladesh floods of
1974 was caused by the saving of lives in the highlands to the
north in the decades before. As for the future, we can confidently say that the more lives are saved in Nepal and Assam the
more lives will be lost in India and Bangladesh. The physical
world is integrated into a system, even if our political world is
not.

Erik Eckholm in *Losing Ground* tells us a number of facts
that should be brought to bear on policy.[4] About 10 percent of
the world's population live in the highlands of the world, and
these people are mostly poor. For geographical reasons, what
this tithe of the world's population does affects 30 percent of
the people. The damage they do is accelerating.

Theoretically we could stop this destruction by shipping
some other form of energy to highland people, say coal or oil.
If oil, we would also have to furnish them with suitable burners,
and there would have to be an efficient distribution system (always a difficult problem in mountainous country). We would
have to persuade them to use the new fuel and to spare their
trees. We would have to change folkways built around the use
of trees: more intervention.

Moreover, we would have to feel that we ourselves could spare
the oil and coal. What chance is there of that? Table 7 throws
some light on this question. With a complete sharing of energy

TABLE 7

Approximate Annual Consumption of Energy in the Mid–1970s
Energy expressed as barrels of oil per capita.

Population	Per capita energy consumption
United States	60
Rich countries	20
World	10
Poor countries	2
India	1
Bangladesh	0.17

throughout the world rich countries as a group would have to give up 50 percent of their present energy consumption; Americans would have to give up 83 percent. We would have to do more than tighten our belts to free that much energy. Our cities and machines are almost irrevocably designed for high energy use. It would take a radical restructuring of our technological civilization to free more than token amounts of energy. But such a restructuring would itself require large amounts of energy! This is but one more of those wretched situations in which we need to lift ourselves by our bootstraps.

Of course there are those who think that Americans are going to have to convert to a less energetic system anyway. I am of that persuasion. Petroleum cannot last much longer, the mining of coal causes serious environmental damage (which can be mitigated only by measures that require energy), and atomic power is dubious. The safety of fission power is limited by the unreliability of human beings;[5] and fusion power now looks less economical than solar power, if indeed it is possible at all.[6]

I have made the point before that the degree of altruism is positively correlated with the wealth of the altruist. Experience also indicates that, for a given level of wealth, the strength of altruism is determined by whether wealth is increasing or decreasing. Of two men both making $20,000 a year the one who made $30,000 last year will not be as generous as the one who has come up from $10,000. With respect to energy it is probable that in the not distant future all the energy-rich nations will enter a period of decreasing energy budgets, and that this period will last as long as the mind can conceive at the present time (more specifically, as long as nations fail to reduce their population sizes). Under these conditions it is unrealistic to expect anything but the merest token gifts of energy from the energy-rich to the energy-poor.

There is only one solution, though it is more theoretical than practical: depopulation of the highlands. If lowlanders will accept the excess, fine; but they probably will not. Even if they did, this move would be only a stop gap measure. Population control at the source is the only real answer. To be self-reliant all countries must sooner or later achieve zero population growth. Overpopulated countries must have negative population growth for a while, with parents averaging fewer than two children per couple. Because of their geography, overpopulated countries in the highlands threaten not only themselves but other sovereignties as well.

Those who live in a rich country like the United States may think that I have spent too much time on this problem of the threat of highland peoples to lowland, because it is a minor threat in the United States and most other rich countries. Although a billion people are threatened almost none of them live in rich countries. But that is precisely why I have spent so much time on this issue—it is an important problem about which we can be objective since we are directly threatened very little by whatever happens. It is a great chance for disinterested altruism, which must, above all, be intelligent. It will not do just to save lives; it is carrying capacity that needs most to be saved, not only for posterity but even for this generation. In fact, I do not see how we can do any good at all unless we make carrying capacity the primary ethical consideration, putting human lives in a subservient position.[7] This conclusion follows not from a contempt for human lives but from a concern for humanity that extends beyond the passing moment of the present.

To many this attitude is unacceptable. For example, John Rawls's highly esteemed *Theory of Justice* pays only lip service to the need for intergenerational justice, being devoted almost entirely to trying to equalize the hands held by everyone in this generation, regardless of the ultimate consequences. I am reminded of the motto of Ferdinand I (1503–1564) of the Holy Roman Empire: *Fiat justitia et pereat mundus* ("Let justice be done, though the world perish"). Of course everyone wants both justice and survival. But suppose, given the constraints, we cannot have both. What then? Which should we choose?

I think our actions should be guided by charity, but I am not willing to settle for the form of charity that has been fashionable in the last half century. I would rather return to an older understanding of the word, to a more bracing form of this necessary virtue. William Davidson, in his essay in the *Encyclopaedia of Religion and Ethics*, says that true charity

> confers benefits, and it refrains from injuring.... Hence, charity may sometimes assume an austere and even apparently unsympathetic aspect toward its object. When that object's real good cannot be achieved without inflicting pain and suffering, charity does not shrink from the infliction.... Moreover, a sharp distinction must be drawn between charity and amiability or good nature—the latter of which is a weakness and may be detrimental to true charity, although it may also be turned to account in its service.[8]

No nation has been dealt so poor a hand that it cannot live

comfortably and be self-reliant at some level of population size and resource use. We deal uncharitably with a nation when we amiably agree that some abstract principle of justice licenses it to ignore the carrying capacity of the land it occupies. Amiability is ruinous not only to distant prospects of posterity but also to the near-term prospects of billions of people now living.

The world is a seamless web in which *we can never do merely one thing.*[9] There is no such thing as an isolated act of charity; to suppose that there is is to commit the sin of amiability. The effects of everything we do spread far beyond the narrow goal our acts are aimed at. If we accept inner responsibility for our acts of altruism we must see to it that they are characterized by more than amiability.[10] If we are not to be ashamed of our actions later we should not commit ourselves to any proposed intervention until we have examined it and convinced ourselves that it deserves the name of true charity. Would-be charitable interventions must be subject to the discipline of environmental impact studies.

6

Survival, the Subtle Assay

THE FINAL CHAPTER is devoted to a discussion of the role of altruism in international relations, but before we can profitably take up that difficult topic we need to dispel certain misconceptions about the nature of survival. We must ask, "Survival of what? And under what conditions?"

Though we can never really know what prehistoric human beings thought about their species as a whole, it is surely most reasonable to assume that there must have been a time when people had no conception of the species to which they belonged. No doubt an individual thought about himself or herself first of all, and to a lesser extent about the members of his family. To a still lesser extent the members of his tribe entered into his decisions, but it is doubtful if other tribes were considered except as competitors or enemies.

The idea of the unity of mankind is one whose origin(s) and development remain yet to be adequately described. For us in Western civilization part of this development took place in the Christian religion. St. Paul, speaking of the covenant between God and his people, wrote that the Scripture describes all mankind as the prisoners of sin, so that the promised blessing might on the ground of faith in Jesus Christ be given to those who have faith. . . . There is no room for "Jew" and "Greek"; there is no room for "slave" and "freeman"; there is no room for "male" and "female"; for in union with Christ Jesus you are all one.[1]

Though this statement asserts the unity of mankind it does so only in the context of religious salvation. It does not say "All humanity is one," but rather that "All humanity can become one—if they accept Jesus." When the Crusaders massacred the Saracens in the Middle Ages, they were not acting inconsistently with Scripture. Equality applied only to those who adopted the true faith. Statements like St. Paul's served very well as a justification of religious imperialism.

The weakening of the bonds of religion in the Renaissance led to a secularization of the idea of the unity of mankind. Gradually voices asserted this unity (and equality) independently of salvation, as we see in a celebrated passage from John Donne (1572–1631):

> No man is an *Iland*, intire of it selfe;
> every man is a peece of the *Continent*,
> a part of the *maine*; if a *Clod* bee
> washed away by the *Sea*, *Europe* is the
> lesse, as well as if a *Promontorie* were,
> as well as if a *Mannor* of thy *friends*
> or of *thine owne* were; any mans
> *death* diminishes *me*, because I am
> involved in *Mankinde*; And therefore
> never send to know for whom the *bell*
> tolls; It tolls for *thee*.[2]

It is beyond my competence to outline the story of the further development of this idea, but I think we can agree that the number of its adherents has become very large in the twentieth century. It seems to be a noble idea; we are attracted to the mutual concern it implies. Yet there are grounds for arguing that accepting it uncritically can lead to actions that are destructive of the ends it supposedly serves, namely, survival in peace and dignity. Much of the modern rhetoric connected with this idea has a biological flavor, e.g., "the brotherhood of man" and "the Family of Man." In fact, even the term *survival* is characteristically biological. In our secularized world, scientific arguments are now used to justify actions that were earlier supported by religion. We need, therefore, to get the biological meaning of survival straight before taking up particular human problems.

The spectre of survival now haunts ethical thought. Attempts to settle the egoism versus altruism issue, to unsnarl population problems, and to lay out the grounds on which international relations can be rationalized all end up with the word *survival*—which is left undefined. It is apparent that not everyone is using the word in the same sense. Within the period of a year books with the contrasting titles of *The Tyranny of Survival*[3] and *The Comedy of Survival*[4] were published. Dip into them where you will; you find the mood and thrust of these books are as different as their titles suggest.

Since Hiroshima ethicists have said that "the modern predicament" centers on the survival issue, but they have not been able to make very clear what they mean by such an assertion. Seeking enlightenment, they have drawn on biology, but that has not helped much because a surprisingly large number of professional biologists are confused. In attempts to devise policy for future actions, survival is introduced as an assay of the wisdom of the proposals. The assay turns out to have subtle characteristics. Three different meanings can be ascribed to the concept of survival, and only one of them leads to a correct analysis.

Most people think that biology tells us that "self-preservation is the first law of life," or words to that effect. The seventeenth-century naturalist John Ray used some such belief as an axiom in refuting van Leeuwenhoek's contention that a sperm cell was the first stage of a new organism. That surely could not be true, said Ray, for the number of sperm cells produced by a single male in his lifetime must "amount to Millions of Millions and so the greatest part of them must needs be lost," producing "the necessary loss of an incredible multitude of them, which seems not agreeable to the Wisdom and Providence of Nature."[5] Here, in implicit form, we see an assumption that surfaces repeatedly in discussions of the implications of biology, the assumption that Nature (or Providence, or God) is an economizer of lives.

The hypothesis of God the Economizer is, I think, one of the intellectual roots of the opposition to elective abortion in our time. Intellectual roots are undoubtedly less important than emotional ones, but they should not be ignored altogether because intellectual roots do, in the heat of argument, supply rationalizations for conclusions already reached by emotional means. As for the facts, the wastage is fantastic. In a population that is not changing in size each two parents produce (on the average) two children. During his lifetime a male can be expected to produce about a million million sperm cells, all but two to four of which perish without achieving what we are pleased to call their "goal." In a woman, the wastage is not quite so spectacular, but it still amounts to perhaps 100,000 ova started on the way to maturation, with at least 400 fully mature and fertilizable egg cells perishing fruitlessly. After the first surprise at learning of this great loss of life most of us find it easy to accept because gametes are, after all, genetically incomplete. Each gamete has only half the double set of chromosomes needed to develop into an adult.

The normal loss of life among chromosomally complete embryos is also substantial and is not generally known. It was only a generation ago that we learned that at least 30 percent of all embryos emplanted in the human uterus are normally and spontaneously aborted; the wastage now seems more likely to be nearer 50 percent.[6] If this fact were widely known and thought about it might lead people to ask themselves this question: "If Nature is not economical of these early lives, why should we be?" I doubt, however, if this question ever comes up at a board meeting of a Right to Life group.

The more we know of Nature the more we realize how profligate she is of lives. But the wastage is not without pattern. As was pointed out in the first chapter, the willingness of a parent to lose his or her life for the sake of the children makes sense. The question is, what sort of sense does it make?

Obviously the survival of the individual is not the *summum bonum*, the "greatest good," in Nature's eyes. As this idea became clear in the nineteenth century, a second interpretation of survival was suggested. Speaking of Nature in his "In Memoriam" Tennyson wrote:

> So careful of the type she seems,
> so careless of the single life. . . .

These words were published ten years before *Origin of Species*. As Darwin's work became widely known—and that happened very rapidly after 1859—this interpretation was developed further. Commentators decided that it was not the preservation of the individual that mattered: it was the preservation of the species. The force called natural selection, they said, selected "for the good of the species." This version is closer to the truth but it is still not close enough. It is, in fact, quite wrong; yet many biologists even today speak and write in these terms. For example, the *Nuffield Biology Teachers' Guide*, written for advanced level (high school) biology teachers in Great Britain includes the following statement: "In higher animals, behavior may take the form of individual suicide to ensure the survival of the species."[7] Many similar statements can be found in textbooks widely used in both Britain and the United States.

Because it is so important that the error of this assertion be fully exposed I am going to attack it twice. I shall ask what look like very simple-minded questions; but if we take these questions seriously we shall uncover some profound insights about the meaning and significance of survival.

First let us ask, "Why a tree?" That is, why does a tree reach up into the sky, towering in some instances a hundred meters above the ground? What is the point of all this height? What good of the species is served by such exuberant growth?

The primary object of any green plant is to intercept the sunlight. The design is most efficient when the plant spreads out widely on the surface of the earth, extending upward as little as possible, no more than is needed to house the necessary thickness of chlorophyll-bearing tissue. One millimeter should be quite enough height for any plant, if it were designed solely for the good of the species. On this fundamental ground it is quite accurate to say that a liverwort clinging to a rock is the noblest work of God the Economizer. But you do not see many liverworts in this world; probably most of my readers do not even know what one looks like. When they think of plants they think of grasses, flowers, bushes, and trees, all of which extend upwards many wasteful centimeters or even meters above the surface of the earth. A tiny amount of productive tissue—the chlorophyll-bearing cells of the leaves—is held aloft by the supporting tissues of stems and trunks, which amount to a hundred or a million times as much mass as that of the photosynthetically productive tissue. Every plant taller than a liverwort is a monument to waste.

Such a monument cannot be explained by selection for the good of the species. It can only be explained by a competitive process in which individuals struggle with each other for a place in the sun. It is wrong to use language that attributes human motives to plants, but expository writing is made easier thereby and no harm is done if the reader recognizes figurative language for what it is. Figuratively speaking, each plant seeking a place in the sun tries to crowd out its fellows by growing upward and spreading out its canopy of leaves at a higher level. Selection constantly favors the plant that can grow highest and fastest, provided its supporting tissues are strong enough to be stable under normally varying conditions. Of course, all language oversimplifies the truth: in the process of winning the primary struggle for a place in the sun the winners create additional eco-logical niches in which plants of a different design can prosper. (At the base of a giant of the forest you are likely to find liver-worts and mosses.)

In passing, it is sobering to realize how much that we prize in the sensual world we owe to the waste that results from com-petitive processes. If selection had in the past acted for the good of the species, the rocks of the world would be covered over only with a paper-thin layer of green; there would be little to tempt the landscape painter. Also there would be no trees and timber in the world—in fact, there never would have been. What would the course of evolution have been for all land-dwelling animals under these conditions? Would human be-ings as we know them have evolved? The mind boggles at trying to imagine an alternative scenario based on selection for the good of the species.

We have already seen that the individual's life may be sacri-ficed for his offspring. What selection favors is, in fact, neither the concrete individual nor the relatively simple abstraction we call the population or the species; what it favors is a subtler abstraction for which we have no better term than *the germ line.*

Language—our language, at any rate—deals awkwardly with time-tied concepts. Unfortunately for clarity of expression, time is of the essence in the selection problem. An individual I can see *now*: so also can I see a population, and perhaps a species. But, a germ line? This abstraction has no terminus in time, and germ lines lose their integrity as they mix together with the passage of time. Yet it is only germ lines that are the "objects" of selection's "attentions." Perhaps Samuel Butler's rhetoric comes as close to the truth as language can: "A hen is only an egg's way of making another egg." Any gene in an egg that improves the efficiency of hens in making more eggs will be selected for. The seed in the pine cone erects a wastefully tall tree just to improve its chances of producing more seeds in pine cones (and to hell with other pine trees!).

Before approaching human problems more closely we need to express clearly and bluntly two great generalizations about the survival problem:

Selection is not, by its nature, for the good of the species.

The survival of the species is an almost accidental by-product of the survival of germ lines.

Now let us ask our second question, "Why a man?" That is, why are human beings as they are? What are the most essential human characteristics? How did evolution bring them into being? And what does this knowledge presage for the future?

It is universally agreed that the most characteristic feature of the human animal is its highly developed brain. In spite of the fact that recent observations of dolphins and apes show more points of similarity between the minds of these species and ours than anyone dreamed of half a century ago, the human mind is still preeminent in its ability to bend the environment to its will. In fact, now that we have learned to split and fuse atoms, we worry that we may have become too successful in manipulating Nature. We may extinguish ourselves. The human mind may prove to be its own undoing.

The central importance of the mind in defining the human species is indicated by our evolutionary history. Going back 14 million years to examine the hominid species that preceded *Homo sapiens*, we find a cranial capacity of about 400 cubic centimeters. Some 11 million years later the cranium was still about the same size. But beginning around 3,000,000 B.C. with *Australopithecus*, cranial capacity rapidly increased until today it is around 1400cc., plus or minus 400cc. (See Figure 3.) At a

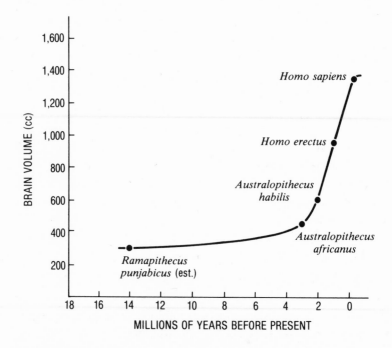

Figure 3. Increase in human brain size over the past 14 million years. After Pilbeam, from Edward O. Wilson (1975), *Sociobiology*, © by Harvard University Press.

conservative estimate, brain capacity has trebled in a mere three million years. In evolutionary terms that is an explosive rate of growth. What caused it?

The exponential upward sweep of the curve suggests an auto-catalytic process, a process in which an effect feeds back into the system to become a cause of more effect. Nothing that we know of the environment outside man during the last three million years suggests a unidirectional cause that could bring about such an explosive growth. We conclude therefore that the brain must have caused its own growth: more exactly, that the competition of one brain with another must have selected for the best brains. (Selection, of course, is to be understood in a strictly Darwinian sense: those with better brains left more descendants than did those with poorer.)

In passing, we must not lose sight of the fact that many concomitant changes had to be coupled with the growth in brain size. The most significant had to do with reproduction and the role of the female in the bearing and rearing of offspring. To permit the birth of a child with a larger brain, the pelvis of the mother had to be modified. There are practical limits to this modification, so birth necessarily became somewhat more dangerous and incapacitating for the mother. As always in evolution, a compromise was struck between opposing goals. But this compromise might have set too low a limit on brain development; it was prevented from doing so by the extension of the periods of juvenile expansibility of the brain case and of juvenile intellectual development. The prolongation of juvenility required a prolongation of parental care, which influenced family structure. These developments were only a few of the accompaniments of increase in brain size.

How could selection have brought about the increase in brain size? What is the selective advantage of being smarter? This question was first asked by people in the intellectual community—scholars, inventors, scientists, professors, and the like. Professional bias made it easy for them to assume that the individual who was smarter (as that term is understood in their community) would be fitter in the Darwinian sense. According to a story attributed to Ralph Waldo Emerson (1803–1882), "If a man builds a better mousetrap than his fellows the world will beat a path to his door, though his house be in the depths of the woods."[8] Early Darwinians lightly assumed that among those tripping up the path would be a bevy of beautiful dolls eager to serve the good of the species by facilitating the proliferation of the mousetrap-builder's genes for inventiveness. By such a social mechanism (it was supposed) the mind of man would evolve to ever greater heights.

Alas! This attractive scenario overlooked one of the simplest of truths: though it may take a genuis to invent a mousetrap any moron can copy it. Invent a better mousetrap and the world will *not* beat a path to your door: it will copy the invention without paying you for it, either in dollars or in dolls.

An invention cannot be widely exploited without the secret of its construction's becoming common knowledge. The information required to reproduce it, like all information, becomes part of the commons. That which is part of the commons cannot reward people differentially, either in economic or in selectionist terms. The inventor-genius gains no selective advantage from his invention once it passes into the commons.

Of course, a contrived advantage may be engineered into the social system. The restrictions of patents and copyrights may be created, but their evolutionary effect will be minor. These social inventions create transferable property rights, and property (together with its advantages) is all too frequently transferred to people whose abilities are quite different from those of the inventor or artist. Patents may do more for the "wheeler-dealer" than they do for the inventor.

That people possessed of what we choose to call genius may not be selectively benefited was first clearly recognized by Darwin's cousin Francis Galton, whose statistical studies showed that "men of eminence" (a mixed bag) had *fewer* than the average number of children, in English society at any rate.[9] Does this fact contradict Herbert Spencer's epitomization of natural selection as "the survival of the fittest"? It depends on how we define the *fittest*. If we define them as whatever genotypes may survive in greater proportion, then Spencer's phrase is true because it is a tautology. But if we define *fittest* according to a criterion other than reproductive success, a characteristic that society holds in high regard, then we will often find that the fittest (so defined) are being slowly eliminated. Whenever that happens the problem of eugenics is created. For a society that has a keen interest in posterity the discovery of a eugenic problem should be very disturbing. For historical reasons our own society is, at present, emotionally unprepared to deal with the eugenic problem, so there is little profit in discussing the matter further. Anyway, we have other fish to fry.

Since the new information created by bright minds passes into a commons, where it cannot create a selective system that favors such minds, we must seek some other explanation for the rapid evolutionary growth of the human brain. Such an explanation has been worked out in the past few decades, principally by Arthur Keith,[10] R. D. Alexander,[11] and Robert Bigelow.[12] Their model is tribalistic; selection distinguishes not so much between individuals as it does between tribes. "The essential characteristic of a tribe is that it should follow a double standard of morality—one kind of behavior for in-group relations, another for out-group."[13] The model is also a highly sanguinary one: it assumes that conflict between tribes was often resolved by the extermination of the loser.

This is not merely an assumption. Read your Bible; read

chapters 10–12 of the book of Joshua for a record of remorseless carnage. A single passage (10:35) can stand for the whole:

> And they took [the city] on that day,
> and smote it with the edge of the
> sword, and all the souls that were
> therein he [Joshua] utterly destroyed
> that day.

This verbal formula is repeated for city after city. Lest the reader miss the full beauty of the massacres, all 31 of the cities devastated by Joshua are listed at the end of chapter 12. This is not the story of a people utterly remote from us—people of a different genetic stock or a different cultural stream—this is the story of our ancestors, our culture. These are our roots. We came from a tribalistic culture. It was brutal. Selection occurred on a tribal basis.

What we know of prehistory fits into the same tribalistic model. Robert Ardrey has brought the general public some appreciation of the very substantial evidence for intraspecies conflict among the australopithecines of Africa.[14] His best-selling books have come in for a great deal of abuse, the reasons for which, it seems to me, are three. First, Ardrey is not an academic; he is a playwright who has made himself thoroughly familiar with the anthropological literature, which he has summarized colorfully—a serious academic sin, and the second reason. Finally, his emphasis on violence as an essential component of human nature grates on the nerves of certain currently powerful opinion makers who assert either that man *is not* violent or that he *should not be*. (It is often not quite clear which they mean.) But the evidence that homicide has been indulged in by human beings for millions of years is overwhelming. It is corroborated by the historical record (see the Bible again).

Corroboration of a different sort is found in the recently learned fact that intraspecific killing occurs in other anthropoids.[15]

Murder was not invented by man. Or perhaps it was. It depends on what one means by the word *murder*, which presents a bothersome semantic problem. In the human context, murder is distinguished from homicide. A homicide is any killing of one member of the species *Homo sapiens* by another member of the same species. If it is an approved-of killing (e.g., capital punishment, the killing of an enemy in war, or the killing of an attacker to save the life of an innocent victim), it is called homicide and nothing more. If the act is disapproved of by the society in which it occurs it is called murder. If, as seems likely, the concept of murder was invented by human beings, then in that sense murder is a human invention. But homicide is known in many species. (Unfortunately, the word *homicide*, derived from the Latin *homo* [man], is etymologically incorrect. "Speciecide" might do, but the word is unknown. Here we have one more instance of linguistic deficiencies that make expository writing difficult.)

Humanitarians of our day often speak of recent wars as being of unparalleled ferocity and destructiveness. If the destruction and loss of life are measured against the size of the population in which they occur this judgment is quite wrong. Modern wars are gentle compared to the tribalistic conflicts of the past. (War as an institution has varied enormously. Sometimes conflict resolution has been almost as formal as jousting, with conventional rather than sanguinary ways of recognizing victory.) It is indubitable that total war was not an invention of the twentieth century: it was merely revived then. It is the winner-take-all conflicts that have the greatest evolutionary consequences. Nearly as great a genetic effect would result from what we might describe as "50 percent total warfare," the recipe for

which was given by Moses when he told his warfaring people
that, besides killing all the adult men among the enemy, they
should:

> kill every male among the little ones, and kill every woman
> that hath known man by lying with him. But all the women
> children, that have not known a man by lying with him, keep
> alive for yourselves.[16]

In other words, kill the men and fertilize the women. It seems
highly probable that this practice was followed for hundreds of
thousands of years. Selection would favor this behavior by conquering males. As for the conquered females, selection would
favor those who acquiesced in the conquest over and against
those who refused to accept their new masters. It is hard to believe that these selective forces could have failed to create fundamental psychological differences between the two sexes (a
consideration that seems not to have occurred to most pro-
ponents of women's liberation).[17]

I think there is no escape from the conclusion that bloody
conflict between groups of men has been a most important selective factor in the evolution of the human mind. This is a
disturbing thought to all who see the elimination of war as a
first priority in the future and who therefore fear any indication
that war might have served a worthy purpose in the past. But
that is no excuse for rewriting history à la 1984. Somewhere, I
believe, T. H. Huxley wrote: "God give me strength to know
the truth even though it destroy me."[18] Is this not the only acceptable attitude among those who claim to be seekers after
truth?

If trees were capable of thought, should a noble tree be
ashamed of its towering beauty because its ancestors brought
it into being by mercilessly wiping out their fellow-trees that
could not grow as fast? Should we be ashamed of our brains

because they blossomed out of massacres and destruction? In any case, the past is not a necessary guide to the future.

The view of the past presented so far is only a partial one. Intertribal conflict and the intertribal genetic selection made possible by total war (or 50 percent total war) easily account for the aggressive component of human behavior. But we are not only aggressive and antagonistic toward one another; quite the contrary, most of the time we act cooperatively and even altruistically. Can we give a plausible explanation for this side of human nature? And can we discern a selective factor powerful enough to account for so rapid an evolution of so large a brain as that of *Homo sapiens*? Such is the first task of our concluding chapter.

7

Brotherhood and Otherhood

MANY PEOPLE HAVE an ambivalent love–hate attitude toward biology. On the one hand they admire the science and like to use its findings to justify beliefs that may have arisen from other sources; on the other they resent the implications of—or at any rate their inferences from—that part of biology that deals with heredity, being ready to cry out "social Darwinism!" whenever selection theory is introduced into the discussion. The admiration of what is supposed to be biology may be as mistaken as the rejection.

It should be clear by now that a belief in the "sanctity of life" finds no support in Nature, if that belief is the justification for cherishing the life of each and every individual human being above all other goods. As far as Nature is concerned, the individual life is cheap, very cheap; Nature (to continue the personification) seeks to conserve something else, something much more subtle. It may be that human policy should indeed be dominated by the concept of the sanctity of life, but if so not with the support of biology.

The eagerness of laymen to denigrate the importance of selection in human affairs may be partly the fault of biologists.

The selection the biologist studies in other animals and plants is almost always genetic selection. Such selection is merely a special instance of a selection that is much broader in meaning. In the human context selection that has no known genetic effect is often of decisive importance. Asking people under stress of need to refrain voluntarily from exploiting a commons that is legally open to them selects for people with weak or nonexistent consciences. Such an assertion neither implies nor denies that conscience can be inherited. This sort of selection is counterproductive of the goals of society independently of the possible genetic basis of conscience, which may not be worth investigating. Among socially interacting human beings we get the behavior we select for. Selection defines the payoff of the rules of society. No assumption about the biology of those rules need be made to predict their consequences. Accompanying the evolutionary progress from early hominids to present-day humankind there has undoubtedly been an increase in the relative importance of non-genetic selection.

We still have to give a plausible reason for the genetic selection of the large human brain. We have seen that the selective advantage conferred by inventiveness with respect to physical artifacts can hardly account for the change in brain size. It is true that the invention of the stirrup gave an advantage to the Mongols for a short while as they swept out of Asia and over Europe;[1] and the longbow gave a momentary but decisive advantage to the English at Crécy; but the ideas embodied in any invention pass speedily into the information-commons, thus soon benefiting nearly everyone equally. That being so, what characteristic might it have been that was genetically selected for so strongly over the past three million years as to produce a trebling of brain capacity in so short a time? I can see only one likely possibility: selection was based on the success of the individual in his role as a tribal member.

Tribal fitness rests on a bipolar virtue: cooperation with tribal brothers coupled with antagonism toward all others. Altruism is selected for, but it is strictly tribal altruism. Until about ten thousand years ago hunting and gathering was the only mode of existence and tribes were small; genetic relations among the members made kin altruism an important selective factor, for the members of a small tribe would possess a considerable degree of genetic relationship. With an increase in the size of the breeding group, particularly if it were combined with certain sorts of exogamy, reciprocal altruism would become relatively more important. This means that purely biological selection diminished in importance in comparison with what we might call social selection.

The total selective value of intratribal altruism was a function of the degree to which a winning tribe was willing and able to exterminate—that is, genetically exterminate—losing tribes. This tribal goal was served by the two-faced virtue of altruism and aggression, intratribal altruism coupled with intertribal aggression. The inward feelings accompanying these orientations may be what we call love and hate. We tend to think of these sentiments as being in opposition to each other, but they are merely two sides of the same coin. It is questionable whether we can have one without the other.[2] Certainly there is ample evidence in fiction (an important depository of psychological truths) for the intensity of one feeling being amplified by the intensity of the other.[3]

What did the bipolar virtue of altruism–aggression select for? Above all else it must have selected for success in communicating within the altruistic group. In all of our relations with our tribal brothers there is a persistent tension between competition and cooperation. One-sided cooperation is not possible, either logically or actually. Language, in the broadest sense, is inescapably ambiguous. In the social setting each of us

needs to read the messages of others correctly under circumstances of almost infinite variability.

Not so long ago Europeans thought that unlettered people
spoke only simple languages of which pidgin English was the
model. Then we discovered that this assumption was far from
the truth: many "primitive" tribes speak languages that are
actually much more complex than ours, and perhaps more
subtle. Though we will never know (in the absence of writing),
it seems highly probable that language was the first great invention of man, that it was, long before writing and agriculture,
brought to a stage of complexity and sophistication comparable
to the finest science of our day. The need for accurate and subtle
communication in a tribe beset by other tribes would select for
brains that could create and manipulate language with skill and
subtlety. Not language itself, but language ability, was genetically selected for. "Language" must not be thought of as verbal
language only: hand gestures, the raising of an eyebrow, and the
pacing of both verbal and nonverbal components all serve the
needs of communication. It is only in the past twenty-five years
that scholars—who tend to be tied to the written word—have
begun to study in depth what actors have known for thousands
of years and prehistoric man probably mastered hundreds of
thousands of years ago.[4] We are just beginning to realize how
little we know (in the scholarly sense) about human communication.

Language ability is of greater selective value than invention
ability for this reason: a captured arrowhead of superior variety
almost reveals the method of its manufacture, but how do you
capture a word on the wing? Vary a dialect ever so slightly and
you create a significant disjunction between people inside the
group and those outside. Complicate communication with gestures, intonations, sarcasm, irony, and other inversions—and
vary these from day to day in a sort of dialectical ballet—and

you create a chasm between in-group and out-group that simply cannot be bridged. If there is one thing we are sure of about communication, it is that spontaneous and rapid speciation of language occurs every time one group splits into two. The power of language speciation is what George Bernard Shaw made such good use of in his *Pygmalion* (on which the musical *My Fair Lady* was based). Language differentiation and tribal identification stand in a mutual cause-and-effect relation to each other. This is the autocatalytic situation that can explain the fantastically rapid evolution of the human brain.

Tribal altruism and intertribal aggression created the mind that is now capable of examining its origins and asking whether the forces of the past must, or should, be equally influential in the future. The human mind can now classify human actions into the opposing categories of egoistic and altruistic. Human beings can pass value judgments on the categories. In their public utterances both the altruist and the egoist generally speak favorably of altruism and unfavorably of egoism—the altruist for obvious reasons, while the egoist (if he is the least bit devious) does so in order to encourage in others the kind of behavior that will benefit him. Such is the peculiarity of dialectic that insures a good press for altruism and a bad one for egoism. A serious investigation must, however, transcend the boundaries of good press relations.

The first chapter asked whether pure altruism is possible. To the theoretician this is a fascinating question, but practical decisions do not have to wait for its answer. Humankind has no doubt always practiced some sort of altruism, behavior that benefited an *alter* somewhat. The question is, "Who is the *alter*?" Must altruism be confined to a small group (like the tribe) or can it include all humanity? There is no accepted scientific or scholarly answer to this question, but there is enough

nique can be called "solving by defining"; it is an invaluable aid
to reformers of whatever stripe.

Neither Calvin nor his followers recognized that in the act
of redefining brotherhood he had in effect destroyed the logical
and emotional heart of the concept. What Calvin had done
was not made clear until three centuries later, when the socialist Pierre-Joseph Proudhon (1809–1865) tore the cover off the
theologian's aphorism. Said Proudhon: "If all the world is my
brother, then I have no brother."[12] There is an essential connection between the warm feeling of brotherhood and the ex-
clusion of others; intimacy is of the essence, as Shakespeare
emphasized in speaking of "we happy *few*." That this heartfelt
warmth is lost in claiming fraternity with a limitless group
has been noted by many people, among them the eighteenth-
century Scottish moralist Adam Ferguson:

> Separation itself has an effect in straitening the bands of so-
> ciety, for the members of each separate nation feel their con-
> nection the more that the name of fellow countrymen stands
> in contradistinction to that of an alien.
>
> In this divided state of the world incompatible interests
> are formed, or at least apprehended; and the members of dif-
> ferent societies are engaged on opposite sides; affection to
> one society becomes animosity to another; and they are not
> always to be reckoned as the most sociable disposition who
> equally fawn upon all.[13]

As evidence of Ferguson's last point consider the revealing
comments of two characters in Dostoyevsky's *The Brothers
Karamazov*:

> "I love humanity," he said, "but I can't help being surprised
> at myself: the more I love humanity in general, the less I
> love men in particular, I mean, separately, as separate indi-
> viduals."[14]

"I must make a confession to you," Ivan began. "I never could understand how one can love one's neighbors. In my view, it is one's neighbors that one can't possibly love, but only perhaps those who live far away."[15]

Dickens treated the matter in a lighter vein in his *Bleak House*. In a chapter significantly entitled "Telescopic Philanthropy" he quotes the words of a Mrs. Jellyby, as she explains to some visitors what she is doing:

"The African project at present employs my whole time. It involves me in correspondence with public bodies and with private individuals anxious for the welfare of their species all over the country. I am happy to say it is advancing. We hope by this time next year to have from a hundred and fifty to two hundred healthy families cultivating coffee and educating the natives of Borrioboola-Gha on the left bank of the Niger."[16]

But when her little boy, Peepy, seeking sympathy, presented himself with bruises and bandages, Mrs. Jellyby could not tear herself away from working for the good of the species, and simply said, "with the serene composure with which she said everything, 'Go along, you naughty Peepy!' and fixed her fine eyes on Africa again."

Telescopic philanthropists sometimes express a pained wonder that less noble mortals are not more impressed with their altruism. But why the preference for intervening in the lives of distant people when so much needs correcting nearer home? The answer is connected with responsibility. As was mentioned without emphasis in chapter 2 (see Table 5) altruism is irresponsible, in the Frankelian sense. Whenever our gain from intervening in the lives of others is unrelated to the good or bad we do to them, our actions are then, strictly speaking, not responsible. Such actions are likely to continue for decades after the nominal reason for them has been subjected to devastating criticism, as happens to be the case with foreign aid.

Like Mrs. Jellyby fixing her fine eyes on Africa, in 1949 the United States, led by President Truman, fixed its fine eyes on the economic and social development of the entire world. Despite the enormous cost of the foreign aid program and the general public disillusionment with it, the program has continued with little diminution for nearly three decades. Why?

In answering that question we must ask another: Who gains what? By now it is widely recognized that many Americans are aided by so-called foreign aid. President Kennedy frankly expressed a selfish national interest on May 26, 1961 when he said, "Foreign aid must become a full partner in American foreign policy." Grants have been made to shore up foreign governments that we hoped would be sympathetic to our national goals. American arms manufacturers have been enriched by the sale of guns and planes at subsidized prices to other countries.

In programs that come closer to what most people like to think of as the goal of foreign aid, our farmers have been made richer by the gift and subsidized sale of so-called surplus grains, a government measure that permitted setting a floor to commodity prices. Railroads and shipping lines made profits from the program. Also benefited were manufacturers of farm machines sold to other countries, which "paid" for them with United States dollars. And the personnel of AID, the Agency for International Development, as well as of that of many private philanthropies focusing on foreign problems, have enjoyed a considerable measure of job security for a long generation. Most of the press releases favoring the continuance of foreign aid are turned out by organizations that have a vested interest in international philanthropy. A vested interest in philanthropy can resist change every bit as much as can a vested interest in business profits.

But all this is to one side of the central question: Is the idea of international altruism fundamentally sound? What do we do when we take upon our own shoulders the problems of another country? Even if we are sure we can solve the material problem that evokes our sympathy we should still hesitate to intervene until we have asked a second and more fundamental question, namely: What does our intervention select for?

At the very beginning of the Revolutionary period in China, Mao Tse-tung committed his country to a policy of *tsu li kong sheng*—"regeneration through one's own efforts."[17] The Chinese have not sought an unrealistic goal of self-sufficiency, but rather one of self-reliance. Such a policy is appropriate to all countries, rich or poor. This policy has made it possible for China to take great strides while similarly needy countries, handicapped by our "help," have lagged behind.

We should assume that every nation has among its cadre of politicians a few like Mao Tse-tung, who cherish self-reliance, together with many more who are perfectly willing to set their countries on the road to permanent parasitism. The more generous rich countries are with their foreign aid the more they strengthen the hands of the latter group. It is surely not without significance that a 1970 survey of the projects proposed to AID by so-called third world countries would, if implemented, have required seven times the world's total energy production.[18] The ideal of self-reliance is, as Thomas Sowell has said,[19] mundane and unfashionable in our time; but perhaps the example of Maoist China will strengthen us to renew our homage to this ancient virtue. Certainly we should seek to make ourselves self-reliant. We should also not be so pusillanimous as to let cries of "Self-serving!" frighten us away from recommending self-sufficiency even to the poorest of countries—especially to the poorest, for it is in the countries that have furthest exceeded the carrying capacity of the land that any policy other than self-reliance is most suicidal.

Yet we continue to fling money desperately at poor countries half a world away, hoping for miracles. In 1975 the United States budgeted 53 million dollars for the republic of Gabon;[20] how many people in America have the slightest knowledge of what the money was supposed to do and what it actually did? Twenty people? I doubt it—though that would be less than 0.00001 percent of our population.

An important appeal of philanthropy is precisely the irresponsibility of it. Telescopic philanthropy is especially appealing because we are unlikely ever to hear of the mistakes we make. We can enjoy believing that we are behaving altruistically without being forced to probe deeper into our motivation.

Reinhold Niebuhr once remarked that "Love for equals is difficult. We love what is weak and suffers. It appeals to our strength without challenging it."[21] The theologian's explanation fits perfectly with the facts of biology. Because we are inescapably egoistic creatures we welcome actions that do not threaten our position in the hierarchy. Philanthropic attention to the weak does not threaten the hierarchical position of the philanthropist; in fact, it may enhance it.

Those who take up telescopic philanthropy because their position in their birthright tribe is ambiguous may presently find themselves surrounded by others who have made the same choice and with whom they can now form a new tribe. In this way they can satisfy the social urge, which is as innate and powerful as egoism. In a prosperous society altruism may even have considerable survival value for the altruist.

It is a humbling experience to realize that one has, during a major part of one's life, pursued a goal that is not only impossible of achievement but, more important, is fundamentally wrong. The pain is made only bearable by the knowledge that a legion of others have made the same mistake.

I am one of those who were born at the time of the First World War and grew up when there was widespread disillusionment with war, with national goals, and even with the idea of nations. Among the more idealistic of this generation disillusionment was tempered by a new vision of a world without walls or barriers of any kind—One World. An obscure poet of the 1920s expressed our yearning well:

> Let us no more be true to boasted race or clan,
> But to our highest dream, the brotherhood of man.[22]

There was no place in our dream for tribes or tribalism. The adjectives *provincial, parochial, insular, territorial, circumscribed, bounded,* and even *patriotic* were simply pejorative. Every step away from regional or group identification was regarded as "a step in the right direction," a spatial metaphor that inadequately takes account of the problem of maintaining a balance in a multidimensional world.

I suppose the majority who were captured by the One World dream in the twenties have awakened by now. In many cases, no doubt, the dream is no longer cherished because monumental difficulties are seen to stand in the way of realizing the goal. Personally, I would put the matter more strongly: the goal is, in the strictest sense, impossible of achievement.

Mere difficulty is insufficient reason for abandoning an ideal. A trip to the moon became possible "in principle" as soon as Newton's *Principia* was published in 1687, though the practical difficulties were so great that it took us 282 years to reach the goal. The dream of One World, however, belongs to a different category, the category of the impossible in principle. The perpetual motion machine is the best-known example of this class, with the Second Law of Thermodynamics serving as the expression of the impossibility, an impossibility so convincing that, as Arthur Eddington said, "if your [alternative] theory is found to be against the Second Law of Thermodynamics I can give you no hope; there is nothing for it but to collapse in deepest humiliation."[23] It is claiming a great deal to put One World in the same basket as perpetual motion machines, but I will defend this claim.

The argument is founded on the nature of competition. Recall the story of the reindeer on St. Matthew Island, discussed in chapter 3. Competition is severe and total whenever members of the same species are brought together into One World, if that world includes no enemies. Violation of the carrying capacity is inevitable for a very simple reason: there is no way that free, egoistically centered individuals, guided by the germ line survival principle, can avoid overwhelming the carrying capacity of their environment. Conceivably some conscientious members of the community might eat less than their share of the food, but the resources they thereby released would soon be absorbed by others with less conscience. Some animals might refrain from reproducing, but the space so freed would soon be occupied by the offspring of those who were less conscientious. A system that depends on free conscience to produce conformity is vulnerable to destruction by the smallest minority of nonconformers. Adapting a phrase of the economist David Ricardo (1772–1823), we can speak of the Iron Law of the Overwhelming Minority. (In fact, his Iron Law of Wages is only a special instance of the larger law.) It is silly to dream dreams of a heaven on earth that presume a value of zero for the size of the disruptive minority.

Wild animals are spared the possibility of committing such foolishness by the blessing of predators—animals of another species whose corrective control of the prey population becomes more intense the more the latter exceeds the carrying capacity. Joseph Townsend (1739–1816) was, in 1786, the first to describe the providential role of predators in his book A *Dissertation on the Poor Laws*.[24]

The potential severity of intraspecific competition is inversely related to the effectiveness of predation. Having gotten rid of almost all our predators (a few micropredators—disease organisms—are not quite conquered), we human beings are deprived of this providential control of our population and must provide some alternative. People who oppose population control by society (e.g., by compulsory sterilization, or the allocation of breeding rights) ask what is intended to be a rhetorical question, "Who is to play God?" But in conquering our predators we have already played God—halfway. If we do not finish the job by replacing predation by social control we shall end in utter misery. We had better take the job of playing God seriously.

A human population living at the very limit of carrying capacity without any social control has been described by the anthropologist Colin Turnbull.[25] For reprehensible reasons that need not concern us here, the government of Uganda uprooted the Iks from their homeland and moved them to an area with far less carrying capacity. The sudden decrease in carrying capacity coupled with the destruction of their social organization speedily produced a group of people—one can hardly call it a society—that was solely governed by egoism. Not only was neighbor pitted against neighbor, but brother against brother, parent against child, and child against parent. Reading Turnbull's eyewitness account is a most unpleasant experience, but one everyone should subject himself to before theorizing about society. The Iks are an incarnation of an aggregation of human animals that, until now, we have thought was no more than a theoretical construct, namely the picture of a society-less people described in the *Leviathan* of Thomas Hobbes (1588–1679):

> During the time men live without a common Power to keep them all in awe they are in that condition called Warre; and such a warre, as is of every man, against every man. For Warre, consisteth not in Battell onely, or the act of fighting: . . . but in the known disposition thereto, during all the time there is no assurance to the contrary. . . .
>
> To this warre of every man against every man, this also is consequent; that nothing can be Unjust. The notions of Right and Wrong, Justice and Injustice have there no place. Where there is no common Power, there is no Law: Where no Law, no Injustice. Force, and Fraud, are in warre, the two Cardinall vertues. Justice and Injustice are none of the Faculties neither of the Body, nor Mind. If they were, they might be in a man that were alone in the world, as well as his Senses, and Passions. They are Qualities, that relate men in Society, not in Solitude. It is consequent also to the same condition, that there be no Propriety, no Dominion, no *Mine* and *Thine* distinct; but only that to be every mans, that he can get; and for so long, as he can keep it.[26]

The descriptions in Hobbes and in Turnbull are especially frightening today because we see such a condition as a likely consequence of total nuclear warfare. Despite all the concern with the life-destroying capabilities of nuclear arms a careful evaluation of the evidence leads to the conclusion that, in the most plausible scenarios, nuclear warfare will be more destructive of human artifacts than it will be of humanity—that is to say, those who survive will find themselves with less wealth and less income per capita. To put the matter another way, the carrying capacity of the earth will suddenly (and for a long time) be much less. With the great loss of life and artifacts there will no doubt be a greater loss of the social and political structure that ordinarily keeps life from becoming "poor, nasty, brutish, and short," in Hobbes's phrase.

What has just been given as an argument for preventing war between sovereign states can be regarded as an argument for trying to create a stateless condition of One World. Paradoxically, however, One World would lead to the same final condition. The people in such a world would still be competitive because the Iron Law of the Overwhelming Minority would insure the persistence of competition. That should not surprise us: we who are alive today are the descendants of an unbroken line of competitive ancestors.[27]

In the absence of competition between tribes the survival value of altruism in a crowded world approaches zero because what ego gives up necessarily (by the definition of the rules of One World) goes into the commons. What is in the commons cannot favor the survival of the sharing impulses that put it there—unless limits are placed on sharing. To place limits on sharing is to create a tribe—which means a rejection of One World. So if we desire a world in which altruism can persist we must reject the ideal of One World and consciously seek to retain a world of more or less separate, more or less antagonistic units called (most generally) tribes. They may be synonymous with nations as we now know them, or they may be some new political inventions. A state of One World, if achieved, would soon redissolve into an assemblage of tribes.

In speaking as I have for a measure of provincialism, parochialism, and patriotism, I do not want to be understood as bestowing unqualified praise on these qualities. That would hardly be consistent with the life I lead. I move in university circles in which many people speak several languages, make frequent trips abroad, and generally have rich social contacts all over the globe. But because this group is no longer confined to a province that can be delineated on a map does not mean that it is utterly free of provincialism of another sort. After all, we have little to do with John Birchers, Fundamentalists, Hollywood stars, or the nobility. (The choice of association is not exclusively ours.) Would we have it otherwise? Certainly not. We happy few, however *we*-ness is defined, require limits to maintain our happy *few*-ness. With at most rare exceptions, men and women require—and seek—a measure of provincialism. (Though, curiously, the obligatory language of their provincialism may include a denial of provincialism.)

The real problem is to define the figurative provinces, together with the means of defending them, in such a way as not to lead to mutual destruction. The ambivalence of tribalism is a destiny we must learn to live with. Because the commons cannot reward virtue, altruism cannot persist if all men are defined as brothers. To nourish altruism a class of brothers must be defined always as considerably less than the class of all men and women. Altruism toward brothers—reciprocal altruism *among* brothers—must be coupled with a measure of antipathy toward others. Our problem—our literally vital problem—is to keep the expression of antipathy within physical bounds that will permit the survival of the species (though not necessarily of all its members). Perhaps this concern for the welfare of the species is the greatest altruism we are capable of.

A world made up of many antagonistic but coexisting tribes, with each individual identifying himself with several tribes of different degrees of inclusiveness, sounds very much like the world we now live in. And so it is; but it is essential that we see that it would be unwise to try to escape this condition. Those who believe that One World is achievable are inclined not to give really serious attention to the problem of *managing* antagonism. Such inattention is increasingly perilous.

Learning to live with error and malfunction is essential to

survival. In the early days of computers, when the components were much less reliable than they are now, the mathematician John von Neumann (1903–1957) pointed out that living organisms achieve a fantastically high degree of reliability despite the fact that the components of which they are composed are rather unreliable. We must, said von Neumann, learn from life: we must take a new look at error. "Our present treatment of error," he said, "is unsatisfactory and *ad hoc*." In the future we must view error

> not as an extraneous and misdirected or misdirecting accident, but as an essential part of the process under consideration—its importance in the synthesis of automata [organisms or computers] being fully comparable to that of the factor which is normally considered, the intended and correct logical structure.[28]

Following von Neumann's lead, computer reliability was rapidly achieved. Redundancy and error-actuated decision functions were the two design elements that nullified the unwanted consequences of inescapable errors.

There is a lesson here. The strategy von Neumann used is unusual in the Western world, particularly in Western science and technology. Rather than try to beat errors out of the system by force, von Neumann said, let us learn how to live with them, let us accept them (in a certain sense).[29] Note the similarity in the dialectic of the following instances:

The acceptance of component error, which makes possible reliability in the design of a living system.

The renunciation of the goal of preserving all the members of a species, demanding no more than germ line survival, which makes possible the survival of the species.

The renunciation of the dream of universal Brotherhood

(because it necessarily degenerates into the fact of universal Otherhood), in favor of many limited brotherhoods, thus making possible the survival of altruism (coupled though it be with limited antagonism).

The dialectic in all three instances should remind us of that in the theological concept of grace—a blessing that cannot be won by force but which can descend as a gift on those who live their lives in the right spirit. The human condition is now such that our population is deprived of providential control by other species, which means that survival under emotionally satisfactory conditions is possible only if we set limits to the practice of altruism. Though we may have attained this insight only with travail, the present is no different from the past; neither can the future be. These truths we must accept.

Notes

1. DOES ALTRUISM EXIST?

1. Ernest Jones (1955), *The Life and Work of Sigmund Freud* (New York: Basic Books), vol.2, pp.60–61.

2. Richard D. Alexander (1967), "The Evolution of Genitalia and Mating Behavior in Crickets (Gryllidae) and Other Orthoptera," *Miscellaneous Publications of the Museum of Zoology, University of Michigan* 133:1–62.

3. Harry W. Power (1975), "Mountain Bluebirds: Experimental Evidence against Altruism," *Science* 189:142–43.

4. George G. Schaller (1972), *The Serengeti Lion: A Study in Predator–Prey Relations* (Chicago: University of Chicago Press).

5. Sarah Blaffer Hrdy (1974), "Male-male Competition and Infanticide among the Langurs (*Presbytis entellus*) of Abu, Rajasthan," *Folia Primatologica* 22:19–58.

6. Hilda M. Bruce (1960), "A Block to Pregnancy in the Mouse Caused by Proximity to Strange Males," *Journal of Reproductive Fertility* 1:96–102.

7. William D. Hamilton (1972), "Altruism and Related Phenomena, Mainly in Social Insects," *Annual Reviews of Ecology and Systematics* 3:193–232. This thorough review includes citations to Hamilton's important earlier work.

8. Robert L. Trivers (1971), "The Evolution of Reciprocal Altruism," *Quarterly Review of Biology* 46:35–57.

9. Edward O. Wilson (1975), *Sociobiology* (Cambridge: Harvard University Press), p.553. This monumental work, a modern classic, is highly recommended for a demonstration of the immense explanatory power of the theory of evolution.

10. Reinhold Niebuhr (1932), *Moral Man and Immoral Society* (New York: Scribner's, 1960), p.55.

11. From Wordsworth's sonnet "Inside of King's College Chapel, Cambridge."

12. Richard M. Titmuss (1970), *The Gift Relationship* (London: Allen & Unwin).

13. Kenneth J. Arrow, "Gifts and Exchanges," in Edmund S. Phelps, ed. (1975), *Altruism, Morality, and Economic Theory* (New York: Russell Sage Foundation).

14. Titmuss, p.14.

15. Ibid., p.12.

16. Ibid., p.13.

17. In John R. Platt (1964), "Strong Inference," *Science* 146: 347–52.

18. Lawrence S. Kubie (1956–57), "Some Unsolved Problems of the Scientific Career," *American Scientist* 41(4), 42(1). Reprinted in Maurice R. Stein, A. J. Vidich, and D. M. White, eds. (1960), *Identity and Anxiety* (Glencoe, Ill.: Free Press), p.255.

19. Ibid., p.252.

20. Titmuss, p.89.

21. George M. Foster (1967), *Tzintsuntzan* (Boston: Little, Brown).

22. Marcel Mauss (1967), *The Gift: Forms and Functions of Exchange in Archaic Societies* (New York: Norton).

23. The importance and danger of envy have been recognized for thousands of years, and yet there seems to be only one book in English devoted to this subject: Helmut Schoeck (1966), *Envy* (New York: Harcourt, Brace & World). This excellent work shows why the subject is necessarily under a general taboo. For observations on the nature of taboo see Garrett Hardin (1973), *Stalking the Wild Taboo* (Los Altos, Cal.: Kaufmann), p.xi.

24. Titmuss, p.72.

25. Ibid., p.89.

26. William Wiser and Charlotte Wiser (1963), *Behind Mud*

Walls, 1930–1960 (Berkeley: University of California Press).

27. Nirad C. Chaudhuri (1951), *The Autobiography of an Unknown Indian* (London: Macmillan).

28. Edward C. Banfield (1958), *The Moral Basis of a Backward Society* (Chicago: Free Press).

29. In Nathan Glazer and Daniel Patrick Moynihan (1967), *Beyond the Melting Pot* (Cambridge: MIT Press), p.195.

30. Banfield, p.18.

31. Langdon Gilkey (1966), *Shantung Compound* (New York: Harper & Row), p.112.

32. Mauss, p.1.

33. Jones, p.389. Unfortunately there are many adults who never progress beyond the stage of the little Freud girl. When such immaturity is combined with intellectual brilliance (as we ordinarily define it) the resulting badly warped character makes us wonder whether we have correctly identified "brilliance." Consider what a friend and student said of Wittgenstein: "He once told me that he had given away his fortune, when a young man, so that he would not have any friends on account of it, but now he feared that he had friends for the sake of the philosophy they could get out of him. He wanted friends who were not trying to *get anything* out of him. Another time he said: 'Although I cannot *give* affection, I have a *great need* for it' "—Norman Malcolm (1958), *Ludwig Wittgenstein. A Memoir* (London: Oxford University Press), p.61. One wonders how Wittgenstein would have commented on Yeats's poem about the girl with the yellow hair.

2. RESPONSIBILITY IN SYSTEMS

1. George Perkins Marsh (1864), *Man and Nature, or Physical Geography as Modified by Human Nature* (Cambridge: Harvard University Press, 1965).

2. William L. Thomas, Jr., ed. (1956), *Man's Role in Changing the Face of the Earth* (Chicago: University of Chicago Press).

3. The analysis of responsibility here given was implicit in Garret Hardin (1968), "The Tragedy of the Commons," *Science* 162: 1243–48. It was first made explicit in tabular form in "Population, Pollution, and Political Systems," in Noël Hinrichs, ed. (1971), *Population, Environment and People* (New York: McGraw-Hill).

The table evolved through several versions. The form given here has not been published before.

4. Adolf Hitler behaved in the same way when, speaking to the Reichstag on 13 July 1934, he justified the massacre of his friend Ernst Roehm and perhaps a thousand other Nazis with these words: "If anyone reproaches me and asks why I did not resort *to* the regular courts of justice, then all I can say is this: In this hour I was responsible *for* the fate of the German people, and thereby I became the supreme judge of the German people" (italics mine)—William L. Shirer (1959), *The Rise and Fall of the Third Reich* (Greenwich, Conn.: Fawcett [n.d.]), p.313.

5. Charles Frankel (1955), *The Case for Modern Man* (New York: Harper), p.203.

6. Garrett Hardin (1963), "The Cybernetics of Competition: A Biologist's View of Society," *Perspectives in Biology and Medicine* 7:58–84. Reprinted in Garrett Hardin (1973), *Stalking the Wild Taboo* (Los Altos, Cal.: Kaufmann).

The properties of privation are not quite as simple as indicated in the text. Because money can earn interest a private enterpriser may be able to make more money in the long run by exhausting a renewable resource and investing the money. If the rate of interest is sufficiently high and the rate of increase of the renewable resource sufficiently low, privatism is as irresponsible to posterity as commonism is. See chapters by Daniel Fife and Colin W. Clark in Garrett Hardin and John Baden, eds. (1977), *Managing the Commons* (San Francisco: W. H. Freeman).

7. Hardin, "The Tragedy of the Commons."

8. See H. V. Muhsam (1973) and Jay M. Anderson (1974), reprinted in Hardin and Baden, *Managing the Commons.*

9. Alfred North Whitehead (1925), *Science and the Modern World* (New York: Mentor, 1948), p.17.

10. In Walter Kerr (1967), *Tragedy and Comedy* (New York: Simon and Schuster), p.105.

11. Joseph Fletcher (1966), *Situation Ethics* (Philadelphia: Westminster).

12. Paul R. Ehrlich and Anne H. Ehrlich (1972), *Population Resources Environment* (San Francisco: W. H. Freeman), p.127.

13. Hardin, "The Tragedy of the Commons."

14. Gregory Bateson, D. D. Jackson, J. Haley, and J. Weakland

(1956), "Toward a Theory of Schizophrenia," *Behavioral Sciences* 1:251–264.

15. Paul Goodman (1968), "Reflections on Racism, Spite, Guilt, and Violence," *New York Review of Books* 10(8):18–23.

16. Matt Herron (1976), "A Not-altogether Quixotic Face-off with Soviet Whale Killers in the Pacific," *Smithsonian* 7(5):22–29.

17. Claude-Adrien Helvétius (1758), *De l'Esprit*; taken, however, from the *Encyclopaedia Britannica* (1974), 6:892.

18. Garrett Hardin (1972), "Exploited Seas—An Opportunity for Peace," *BioScience* 22:695.

19. Garrett Hardin (1976), "Fishing the Commons," *Natural History* 85(7):9–15.

20. James A. Wilson (1977), "A Test of the Tragedy of the Commons," in Hardin and Baden, *Managing the Commons*. An interesting account of how Maine lobstermen wrestle with the problem of the commons.

3. ETHICAL IMPLICATIONS OF CARRYING CAPACITY

1. Jonathan B. Bingham (1953), *Shirt-Sleeve Diplomacy, Point Four in Action* (New York: John Day), pp.10ff.

2. The Paddock brothers were, so far as I know, the first to call attention to this series of euphemisms. Like the little boy who identified the emperor's new clothes they received no credit for their public service. See William Paddock and Paul Paddock (1964), *Hungry Nations* (Boston: Little Brown), p.18.

3. W. W. Rostow (1960), *The Stages of Economic Growth: A Non-Communist Manifesto* (London: Cambridge University Press).

4. For a knowledgeable discussion of the complexities of the problem see John M. Culbertson (1971), *Economic Development: An Ecological Approach* (New York: Knopf).

5. David R. Klein (1968), "The Introduction, Increase, and Crash of Reindeer on St. Matthew Island," *Journal of Wildlife Management* 32:350–67.

6. Charles S. Elton (1958), *The Ecology of Invasions by Animals and Plants* (London: Methuen), p.148.

7. Susan L. Flader (1974), *Thinking Like a Mountain* (Columbia: University of Missouri Press). The title of this life of Aldo

Leopold is derived from an essay of the same title, which he wrote in 1944. In Leopold's mind, "thinking like a mountain" meant thinking ecologically, seeing the whole picture.

8. China has not taken a census of its people since the mid–1950s. The present population is estimated to be between 750 million and 980 million. Much has been made of this uncertainty by the outside world, with the implication that the Chinese leaders could plan better if they knew the exact population. But perhaps these leaders, like Leopold, are reading the signs in terms of carrying capacity. If so, it is doubtful if the quality of their planning would be improved by an accurate census.

9. People who have never watched a predator "spooking" a herd of prey to see which ones behave abnormally do not appreciate how selective predators are. In a battle over the wolf question in Minnesota the secretary of a sportsman's association sarcastically asked, "What do the wolves do? Give the deer medical exams before killing them?" As it happens, that is precisely what they do. See John G. Mitchell (1976), "Fear and Loathing in Wolf Country," *Audubon* 78(3):20–39.

10. Farley Mowat (1963), *Never Cry Wolf* (New York: Dell).

11. Friedrich Engels (1844), "Outlines of a Critique of Political Economy," in Ronald L. Meek, ed. (1953), *Marx and Engels on Malthus* (London: Lawrence and Wishart), p. 58.

12. Harrison Brown (1954), *The Challenge of Man's Future* (New York: Viking), chap.7.

13. George Stewart shrewdly saw this point and made use of it in his moving and interesting novel, *Earth Abides* (New York: Random House, 1949).

14. As a molder of public opinion the biologist Paul R. Ehrlich deserves great credit for writing *The Population Bomb* (New York: Ballantine, 1968), a superb example of journalistic writing at its best.

15. Karl Marx (1875), Critique of the Gotha program. Reprinted, *inter alia*, in R. C. Tucker, ed. (1972), *The Marx–Engels Reader* (New York: Norton).

16. Garrett Hardin and John Baden, eds. (1977), *Managing the Commons* (San Francisco: W. H. Freeman). See the essay "What Marx Missed."

17. Garrett Hardin (1974), "Living on a Lifeboat," *BioScience* 24:561–68. This article was the first ecological analysis of the world food bank proposal. Reprinted in Hardin and Baden, *Managing the Commons*.

18. Piers Paul Read (1974), *Alive* (New York: Avon), pp.81–82.

19. M. Taghi Farvar and John P. Milton, eds. (1972), *The Careless Technology* (Garden City, N.Y.: Natural History Press), chap. 13 by Thayer Scudder, pp.206ff.

20. Ibid., chap.23 by Teodoro Boza Barducci, pp.423ff.

4. WHO CARES FOR POSTERITY?

1. John Trumbull (1782), "McFingal," canto II, lines 121ff. Reprinted in Edwin T. Bowden, ed. (1962), *The Satiric Poems of John Trumbull* (Austin: University of Texas Press), p.129.

2. Hans Jonas (1974), *Philosophical Essays* (Englewood Cliffs, N.J.: Prentice-Hall).

3. Martin Buber (1970), *I and Thou* (New York: Scribner's).

4. John Rawls (1971), *A Theory of Justice* (Cambridge: Harvard University Press). See especially pp.284–93.

5. Rawls has become the darling of the liberal-to-radical branch of the political spectrum of our time; his theory of "justice as fairness" fits in perfectly with their political aims. Many professional philosophers, however, have not been taken in by Rawls. See Brian Barry (1973), *The Liberal Theory of Justice* (Oxford: Clarendon Press). See also vol.3, no.1 of *Social Theory and Practice* (1974), a special issue devoted to Rawls. One is struck by the frequency with which a critical reviewer begins by identifying A *Theory of Justice* as "a work of major importance," or speaks of "my great respect for the author," before proceeding to dismember Rawls's argument, enthymeme by enthymeme. Charles Frankel is more forthright. In his essay "Justice, Utilitarianism, and Rights" (1974), *Social Theory and Practice* 3(1):27–46, Frankel says that Rawls's work is "not so much argument as atmospherics," and remarks that his prose "gives off that special aroma of diffident perplexity which has become, these days, the seal of good housekeeping in philosophy." Still more strongly Frankel states that "the confusion between fact and faith is not merely incidental in Rawls's argument, but indis-

pensable to it." In the light of all the justifiable criticism that has been leveled against it the puzzle is why the popular–intellectual press—magazines like the *New York Review of Books*—treat Rawls with such awe. This is a problem in the sociology of the knowledge industry.

6. M. Taghi Farvar and John P. Milton, eds. (1972), *The Careless Technology* (Garden City, N.Y.: Natural History Press). See particularly the article by Carl J. George.

7. Garrett Hardin, "Why Plant a Redwood Tree?" in G. Tyler Miller (1975), *Living in the Environment* (Belmont, Cal.: Wadsworth).

8. Garrett Hardin (1974), "The Rational Foundations of Conservation," *North American Review* 259(4):14–17.

9. Raymond Swing (1964), *Good Evening* (New York: Harcourt, Brace & World), p.137.

10. Jack R. Harlan (1975), "Our Vanishing Genetic Resources," *Science* 188:618–21.

11. Ancel Keys et al. (1950), *The Biology of Human Starvation* (Minneapolis: University of Minnesota Press).

12. H. S. Guetzkow and P. H. Bowman (1946), *Men and Hunger* (Elgin, Ill.: Brethren Publishing House).

13. St. Thomas Aquinas, *Summa Theologica*, translated by the Fathers of the English Dominican Province (New York: Benziger Bros., 1947), vol. 1, p.1022.

14. George Berg (1968), "Environmental Pollution in the Inner City," *Scientist and Citizen* 10(5):123–25.

15. Edmund Burke (1790), *Reflections on the Revolution in France* (Garden City, N.Y.: Doubleday, 1961) p.45.

16. Melford E. Spiro (1956), *Kibbutz: Venture in Utopia* (Cambridge: Harvard University Press). The author tells how children brought up in a spartan, communal kibbutz, in which there is very little that can acquire the emotional aura of "home," develop emotional attachments to such fixed natural objects as trees.

17. Kenneth E. Boulding, "Commons and Community: The Idea of a Public," in Garrett Hardin and John Baden (1977), *Managing the Commons* (San Francisco: Freeman). Boulding makes this point forcefully, giving the mathematical theory on which it is based.

5. WHO DEALT THIS HAND?

1. The statements made about China are based on estimates by the FAO (the Food and Agricultural Organization of the United Nations) and our CIA. It is distressingly difficult to find solid facts. China's understandable reluctance to publish statistics is made worse by our stupidity. For years the FAO statistics lumped figures for Chiang Kai-shek's Taiwan and Mao's China, no doubt in response to pressure from the United States, which did not recognize mainland China.

There may have been good diplomatic reasons for the nonrecognition of communist China that went on for a quarter of a century —though I confess I was never able to understand what they might be—but it was utter stupidity to destroy information by confounding data from the opposing regimes. Even granting the validity of insisting that mainland China (with over 900 million people) was merely an obstreperous appendage of Taiwan (with its 16 million), we still had excellent reasons for wanting to know the import-export balances of the two regions separately.

2. Anthony C. Picardi and William W. Seifert (1976), "A Tragedy of the Commons in the Sahel," *Technology Review* 78(6):42–51.

3. Garrett Hardin (1971), "Nobody Ever Dies of Overpopulation," *Science* 171:527.

4. Erik P. Eckholm (1976), *Losing Ground* (New York: Norton).

5. Garrett Hardin (1976), "The Reliability Factor," *Skeptic* no. 14:10–13, 45–46. The entire issue is on atomic power and balances pro and con articles nicely. See also Garrett Hardin (1976), "Living with the Faustian Bargain," *Bulletin of the Atomic Scientists*, 32(9):25–29. See also counter-arguments by Alvin M. Weinberg in the same issue.

6. Philip H. Abelson (1976), "Glamorous Nuclear Fusion," *Science* 193:279.

7. Garrett Hardin (1976), "Carrying Capacity as an Ethical Concept," *Soundings* 59(1):120–37.

8. William L. Davidson (1928), "Charity," in *Encyclopaedia of Religion and Ethics* (New York: Scribner's), vol.3, p.373.

9. Garrett Hardin (1972), *Exploring New Ethics for Survival:*

The Voyage of the Spaceship Beagle (New York: Viking), chap.5.

10. It should be apparent that much of the distinction between amiability and charity is essentially one of short-term versus long-term benefits and costs, and this balance fits into the posterity problem. James M. Buchanan has treated it under the heading of "compassion" in his analysis of "The Samaritan's Dilemma," in Edmund S. Phelps, ed. (1975), *Altruism, Morality, and Economic Theory* (New York: Russell Sage Foundation).

6. SURVIVAL, THE SUBTLE ASSAY

1. "The Letter to the Galatians," 3:22, 28, in Edgar J. Goodspeed (1948), *The Complete Bible, an American Translation* (Chicago: University of Chicago Press), p.178.

2. John Donne (1624), "Devotion XVII," in *The Complete Poetry and Selected Prose of John Donne & the Complete Poetry of William Blake* (New York: Modern Library, 1946), p.332.

3. Daniel Callahan (1973), *The Tyranny of Survival* (New York: Macmillan).

4. Joseph Meeker (1974), *The Comedy of Survival* (New York: Scribner's).

5. John Ray (1721), *Three Physico-Theological Discourses*, 4th ed. (London: William & John Innys), p.59.

6. Carl G. Hartman (1962), *Science and the Safe Period* (Baltimore: Williams and Wilkins).

7. Richard Dawkins (1976), *The Selfish Gene* (New York: Oxford University Press), p.9.

8. The quotation is not quite what Emerson said. We are confronted with an instance in which those who have written glosses on the master's words have effected an improvement. See *Familiar Quotations by John Bartlett*, 13th ed. (Boston: Little, Brown, 1955), p.504, col. b.

9. Francis Galton (1869), *Hereditary Genius* (New York: Appleton, 1870).

10. Arthur Keith (1949), *A New Theory of Human Evolution* (New York: Philosophical Library).

11. Richard D. Alexander (1971), "The Search for an Evolutionary Philosophy of Man," *Proceedings of the Royal Society of Victoria* 84(1):99–119.

12. Robert Bigelow (1969), *The Dawn Warriors* (Boston: Little, Brown).

13. Garrett Hardin (1971), "Population, Biology and the Law," *Journal of Urban Law* 48:563–78. Reprinted in Garrett Hardin (1973), *Stalking the Wild Taboo* (Los Altos, Cal.: Kaufmann).

14. Robert Ardrey (1961), *African Genesis* (New York: Atheneum); and Ardrey (1967), *The Territorial Imperative* (New York: Atheneum).

15. Edward O. Wilson (1975), *Sociobiology* (Cambridge: Harvard University Press). See entries under *murder* and *infanticide*. The epithet *murder* is inappropriate for reasons discussed in the text.

16. Numbers 31:17–18.

17. Langdon Gilkey (1966), *Shantung Compound* (New York: Harper & Row). On pp.211–12 is an account that is highly relevant to this question, though hardly decisive. Toward the conclusion of the Second World War a rescue squad of seven American soldiers took over the prison camp, ruling it until liberation was safe. Says Gilkey: "These seven men who ruled the camp for the next two weeks, were like gods among us. They were, in fact, as a group, large in physique, handsome, and capable ... so different from the shrunken humanity" of the prison camp. Men and women prisoners of all ages and conditions kowtowed to the liberators. But it was "the women of the camp who most instinctively recognized their divine status. Of all ages, whether from high society or low, married or single, proper or not so proper, all wanted nothing better than to adore. They followed the pleasantly surprised soldiers everywhere, staring at them, fighting for the chance to wait on them, and pushing their equally adoring children aside so as to be able slyly to touch or stroke them. As always, it was wonderful to have gods in your midst—unless, like the writer and a few others, you lost a girl friend in the process!"

The "gods" were allies rather than enemies, so it cannot confidently be said that these women would have shown the same adoration toward conquerors; yet there is considerable anecdotal evidence from war histories to show that many women do shift their allegiance when the victory of the enemy is perceived as total. The proportion of women who change over has been small in recent years, perhaps because under modern conditions of communication even a decisive battle may not be perceived as the end of a war.

Of course it is not all certain that there is any difference between men and women. See Stanley Milgram (1974), *Obedience to Authority* (New York: Harper & Row). In only a small series of experiments Milgram found no difference between men and women in their obedience to authority. In the classical 50 percent warfare only women have a chance to benefit by their acquiescence; but whatever genes they might have for this behavior would be passed on to both sexes. The question is, would the expression of these genes be sex-limited (as is true of the genes for beards, for instance)? The answer is not known. The present climate of opinion is unfavorable for investigating questions like this.

18. I am unable to find the source of this quotation in my files. Have I imagined it? The flavor is certainly Huxleyan, and so I use it—even though I may be deviating from the truth in attributing it to him. (Only the inclusion of this note salves my conscience!)

7. BROTHERHOOD AND OTHERHOOD

1. Lynn Townsend White (1962), *Medieval Technology and Social Change* (Oxford: Clarendon Press).

2. The bearing of tribalism on the semantics of ethics is well expressed in Robert Bigelow (1969), *The Dawn Warriors* (Boston: Little, Brown), p.58: "There is no sharp line between 'good' and 'evil,' and . . . cooperation, communication, courage and love are very closely related indeed to conflict, deception, terror, and hatred. . . . Every increase in the size of the brain was produced by the mixed emotions of love and ferocity."

3. We should note the psychoanalytic insight that the opposite of love is not hate but indifference. "I hate you!" gives the lover hope; "I couldn't care less" removes all hope. Love and indifference cannot both be directed toward the same person. Love and hate can: the result is generally a stormy relationship. When love and hate are directed at different targets each intensifies the other and the mixture produces the euphoria out of which heroic literature has grown. It may have been an appreciation of this inner feeling that led a Spanish philosopher to say, "There is much more humanity

in war than in peace"—Miguel de Unamuno (1912), *The Tragic Sense of Life* (New York: Dover, 1954), p.279.

4. Michael Argyle and Mark Cook (1976), *Gaze and Mutual Gaze* (New York: Cambridge University Press). A reviewer of this book (*Science* 194:54) remarks: "Within conversations, the patterning gaze is intimately linked to the tempo of speech and gesture, producing an interactional pattern of incredible complexity." See also the following works: Erving Goffman (1959), *The Presentation of Self in Everyday Life* (New York: Doubleday); and Edward T. Hall (1966), *The Hidden Dimension* (New York: Doubleday).

5. I have never read the entire Bible, so I rely here on the authority of a friend who, I trust, has: Kenneth E. Boulding (1953), *The Organizational Revolution* (New York: Harper), pp.78–79.

6. Deuteronomy 23:20.

7. Benjamin Nelson (1969), *The Idea of Usury: From Tribal Brotherhood to Universal Otherhood*, 2d ed. (Chicago: University of Chicago Press).

8. William Shakespeare (1599), *King Henry V*, act 4, sc.3, 1.60.

9. Nelson, p.79.

10. Ibid., p.81.

11. Ibid., p.81n.

12. Alexander Gray (1946), *The Socialist Tradition* (London: Longmans, Green), p.159; the original source is not given.

13. Adam Ferguson (1792), *Principles of Moral and Political Philosophy*. Quoted in Louis Schneider (1967), *The Scottish Moralists on Human Nature and Society* (Chicago: University of Chicago Press), p.86.

14. Fyodor Dostoyevsky (1880), *The Brothers Karamazov* (Baltimore: Penguin Books), vol.1, p.62.

15. Ibid., vol.1, p.276.

16. Charles Dickens (1853), *Bleak House* (New York: New American Library, 1964), chap.4, pp.53–54.

17. *Eastern Horizon*, vol.9, no.3, pp.8–24 (1945).

18. Miles Copeland in a letter to *The Times* (London), 21 December 1973.

19. Thomas Sowell (1975), *Race and Economics* (New York: McKay), p.238.

20. *Foreign Affairs Newsletter* 1(4):2 (1974). Gabon was only one of the 94 countries receiving foreign aid in that year. The figure lumps military and technical aid.

21. Reinhold Niebuhr (1937), *Beyond Tragedy* (New York: Scribner's), p.155.

22. Thomas Curtis Clark, "The New Loyalty," in Thomas Curtis Clark and Esther A. Gillespie, eds. (1927), *The New Patriotism* (Indianapolis: Bobbs-Merrill).

23. A. S. Eddington (1928), *The Nature of the Physical World* (New York: Macmillan), p.74.

24. Joseph Townsend (1786), *A Dissertation on the Poor Laws* (Berkeley: University of California Press, 1971). Townsend tells the story of the population of goats on Robinson Crusoe's island, San Fernandez, off the coast of Chile, before and after the introduction of a providential colony of predatory hounds. It is a pity that so fundamental an insight into population dynamics should take so long to penetrate the general consciousness: had the men who introduced the deer to St. Matthew Island (chap.3, note 5) known of Townsend's work they could have avoided their devastating error.

25. Colin M. Turnbull (1972), *The Mountain People* (New York: Simon and Schuster).

26. Thomas Hobbes (1651) *Leviathan* (New York: Dutton, 1950), pp.103, 105.

27. Our unwillingness to take competition seriously is due, apparently, largely to the effectiveness of sociologists in determining the climate of opinion. See chapter 19 of Garrett Hardin (1977), *Stalking the Wild Taboo*, 2d ed. (Los Altos, Cal.: William Kaufmann).

28. John von Neumann (1956), "Probabilistic Logics and the Synthesis of Reliable Organisms from Unreliable Components," in *Collected Works* 5:329–78 (New York: Macmillan, 1963), p.329.

29. After von Neumann's death the development of solid-state physics made possible the manufacture of computer components of so high a degree of reliability that his strategy is now hardly needed—for computers. But I know of no evidence that the political reliability of *Homo sapiens* has improved, or is likely to do so.

Index